Born Free

Born Free

How to Find Radical Freedom
and Infectious Joy
in an Authentic Faith

Steve Brown

A Raven's Ridge Book

Baker Books
A Division of Baker Book House Co
Grand Rapids. Michigan 49516

Scripture quotations unless otherwise marked, are taken by permission from The New King James Version, copyright © 1979, 1980, 1982, Thomas Nelson, Inc., Publishers.

Scripture quotations marked NIV are taken from the HOLY BIBLE, NEW INTERNATIONAL VERSION®. NIV®. Copyright © 1973, 1978, 1984, International Bible Society. Used by permission of Zondervan Publishing House.

The Scripture quotation marked NASB is taken by permission from the New American Standard Bible, © 1960, 1962, 1963, 1968, 1971, 1973, 1975, 1977, The Lockman Foundation, La Habra, California.

ISBN: 0-8010-1069-1

Second printing, August 1994

Printed in the United States of America

Contents

Acknowledgments

This is a different kind of book for me.

I didn't just sit down and create a typed manuscript. Rather, I stood in front of seminar audiences and taught from my heart the message I believe I was born to teach: that true faithfulness flows naturally from God's gifts of freedom, joy, and grace. This book was taken from transcripts of those seminar messages.

There was a lot of freedom in the way I said things in those seminars and, because this book was taken from seminar transcripts, you are going to have to exercise a lot of grace in reading it. Public speaking is different from putting one's thoughts on paper. (See my book, *How to Talk So People Will Listen*, published by Baker Books. That, of course, is a shameless effort at self-promotion. I'm not above that.)

My writing and speaking is always colloquial in style. However, a book taken from a transcription reflects a colloquial style that goes far beyond anything I have done in previous books. If that offends, I ask your forgiveness. They made me do it. If you like it better, it was the result of my great wisdom in deciding to do it this way.

Key Life Network, the ministry in which I serve, conducts "Born Free" seminars in cities all over America. If you would like information on those seminars, you can call 1-800-KEY LIFE. (That, of course, is a commercial. I'm not above that, either.) Much of the material in this book, *Born Free*, and in the next one, *Living Free*, is taken and will be taken from those two seminars.

Three of my friends and colleagues—recording artist Buddy Green, and dramatists Charlie and Ruth Jones (better known as "Peculiar People")—are an integral part of the pedagogical process of the Born Free seminars. Without their music and drama, a lot of the seminars' impact is lost.

Creating a book from a seminar transcript requires a person of great sensitivity and talent. That person is Bill Deckard, whose significant gifts of editing, writing, and clarifying are appreciated more than he knows.

And while I'm thanking people, I want to thank my wife, Anna, whose love, prayers, godliness, encouragement, and occasional admonishment is the "wind beneath my wings"; Cathy Wyatt, Key Life's vice president of marketing, who has been responsible for much of what has happened in the Born Free seminars; Richard Farmer, Key Life's executive vice president, whose friendship and direction have, on more than one occasion, prevented me from making a fool of myself; Robin DeMurga, who oversees everything I write and say, to make sure that it is "proper" and cogent; Steve Griffith, my friend, editor, and representative to the publishers; and the entire staff at Key Life—Bonnie, Beth, Bryce, Carolyn, Dick, and all the volunteers—who make possible everything I do.

To them (and to so many others too numerous to mention) I offer my heartfelt thanks. This book would have been far worse without them . . .

. . . but then again, maybe it could have been better.

Introduction

Then Jesus said to those Jews who believed Him, "If you abide in My word, you are My disciples indeed. And you shall know the truth, and the truth shall make you free." . . . Therefore if the Son makes you free, you shall be free indeed. (John 8:31–32, 36)

Up front I want you to know that, if you are not a Christian, if you are not "born again," if you are not in a relationship with Jesus Christ, this book is not for you. It just ain't gonna work. But even if you are a Christian, if you don't know the truth you won't experience the radical freedom and infectious joy this book's cover promises.

Telling you the truth is what this book is all about.

As you read *Born Free*, expect to be faced with the truth in a number of ways. First, expect *doctrinal* truth. I believe there are facts, revealed propositional truths, that Christians need to know. Hopefully, it won't put you to sleep, but if you read much farther you will be receiving some doctrinal truth.

You can also expect to hear my own *experiential* truth. I believe that one of the reasons God called me to do what I do is so that Christians can say, "If Steve Brown can do it, anybody can do it." I'm going to be as honest with you as I can be about the places where I've been successful, but I'm also going to be as honest as I can be about the places where I've failed. Being free isn't for super-Christians. It's for ordinary Christians like you and me.

You will also face some *painful* truth. As we move out of some of the areas of denial that we as Christians build around ourselves, and as we begin to look at ourselves the way we really are, there is going to be some pain. There may even be some tears, but that is part of what it's all about.

You can also expect *joyful* truth. As we take our journey toward freedom, there will be a sense of the world being lifted off your shoulders. A sense of joy and excitement and reality that most of us—and I include myself—haven't felt in a very long time.

Finally, it is my prayer as you read this book (or participate in a Born Free seminar), that you will face *your* truth. It is very important as you go through this material that you be honest before yourself and epecially before God.

I believe Psalm 102:18-22 is a prophetic psalm for each of you who is reading this book. This is what the psalmist says:

> This will be written for the generation to come,
> That a people yet to be created may praise the LORD.
> For He looked down from the height of His sanctuary;
> From heaven the LORD viewed the earth,
> To hear the groaning of the prisoner,
> To release those appointed to death,
> To declare the name of the LORD in Zion,
> And His praise in Jerusalem,
> When the peoples are gathered together,
> And the kingdoms, to serve the LORD.

The promise of the entire Old Testament, for those who live in our time, is that we would be free. That the burden of the law would be lifted. That we might find the place to laugh the laughter of the redeemed. Jesus came to fulfill that prophecy.

Jesus himself declares this in Luke 4:16-21:

> So He came to Nazareth, where He had been brought up. And as His custom was, He went into the synagogue on the Sabbath day, and stood up to read. And He was handed the book of the prophet Isaiah. And when He had opened the book, He found the place where it was written:
>
> > The Spirit of the LORD is upon Me,
> > Because He has anointed Me to preach the gospel to the poor;

He has sent Me to heal the brokenhearted,
To proclaim liberty to the captives
And recovery of sight to the blind,
To set at liberty those who are oppressed;
To proclaim the acceptable year of the LORD.

Then He closed the book, and gave it back to the attendant and sat down. And the eyes of all who were in the synagogue were fixed on Him. And he began to say to them, "Today this Scripture is fulfilled in your hearing."

Jesus didn't come to make you holy (though holiness is good). Jesus didn't come to sanctify you, (though you ought to be involved in the process of sanctification). Jesus didn't come to make you a good church member. He didn't come to teach you and others to know Him. *Jesus came to set you free*, to allow you to laugh, to allow you to be free of the prisons that even religion will put you in. Your heritage is freedom.

Despite that heritage, despite the reality that that's what God was all about when He sent His son into the world— *most of us aren't free.* If we're honest with ourselves, we know that many of us became less free when we became a Christian. For twenty-eight years I've listened to Christians come to my study and say, "I remember when I didn't know Him . . . and I was happier then."

I'm going to ask you as you read this book to face the reality that sometimes, after we came to know Him, we find ourselves more bound than we were before.

1

The Twelve Most Common Christian Prisons

Let the groaning of the prisoner come before You;
According to the greatness of Your power
Preserve those who are appointed to die. (Psalm 79:11)

Do you ever feel like that? Even though you believe that in Christ you are free, do you feel like a prisoner? While expectantly looking forward to eternal life, do you feel "appointed to die"? In this first chapter we are going to explore some of the prisons in which Christians often find themselves. We sometimes think that grace is needed only by pagans and certainly not by Christians. I want to show you some ways in which Christians, no less than unbelievers, can live in prison.

In *The Last Battle*, the final book of the classic Narnia series by C. S. Lewis, Lucy asks Aslan the lion, who represents Christ, the Lion of Judah, to help some dwarfs. The dwarfs are already inside Narnia, which represents heaven, but they think that they are still back on earth in a stable. They refused to see the beauty of Narnia. Lucy says, "Aslan, could you—will you—do something for these poor Dwarfs?"

And Aslan replies, "Dearest, . . . I will show you both what I can, and cannot, do." And then we read,

He came close to the Dwarfs and he gave a long growl: low, but it set all the air shaking. But the Dwarfs said to one another, "Hear that? That's the gang at the other end of the Stable. Trying to frighten us. They do it with a machine of some kind. Don't take any notice. They won't take us in again!"

Aslan raised his head and shook his mane. Instantly a glorious feast appeared on the Dwarfs' knees: pies and tongues and pigeons and trifles and ices, and each Dwarf had a goblet of good wine in his right hand. But it wasn't much use. They began eating and drinking greedily enough, but it was clear that they couldn't taste it properly. They thought they were eating and drinking only the sort of things you might find in a Stable. One said he was trying to eat hay and another said he had got a bit of an old turnip and a third said he'd found a raw cabbage leaf. And they raised golden goblets of rich red wine to their lips and said, "Ugh! Fancy drinking dirty water out of a trough that a donkey's been at! Never thought we'd come to this." But very soon every Dwarf began suspecting that every other Dwarf had found something nicer than he had, and they started grabbing and snatching, and went on to quarreling, till in a few minutes there was a free fight and all the good food was smeared on their faces and clothes or trodden under foot. But when at last they sat down to nurse their black eyes and their bleeding noses, they all said:

"Well, at any rate there's no Humbug here. We haven't let anyone take us in. The Dwarfs are for the Dwarfs."

"You see," said Aslan. "They will not let us help them. They have chosen cunning instead of belief. Their prison is only in their own minds, yet they are in that prison; and so afraid of being taken in that they can not be taken out. But come, children. I have other work to do."[1]

The dwarfs were in a totally unnecessary prison—a prison of the mind; a prison that Aslan, and Jesus, never intended.

We're going to look at twelve common prisons that I have seen myself or others get trapped in over my years as a pastor and Bible teacher. I have divided these twelve prisons into four groups. The first group is prisons of what we do:

the prison of sin, the prison of guilt, and the prison of failure.

The second group is prisons formed by what we think: the prison of the past, of self-abasement, and of perfectionism.

Third is the prisons of how we relate to others: the prison of fear, of needing approval, and of obligation.

Finally we will examine the prisons of how others control us: the prison of rules, of religion, and of "gurus."

The Prisons of What We Do

So let's begin by considering the first prison of what we do—*the prison of sin*. The Old Testament prophet Isaiah knew about this kind of prison:

> Behold, the LORD's hand is not shortened,
> That it cannot save;
> Nor His ear heavy,
> That it cannot hear.
> But your iniquities have separated you from your God;
> And your sins have hidden His face from you,
> So that He will not hear. (Isaiah 59:1–2)

Do you ever feel like that? Do you ever feel that there is a great wall separating you from God? Could it be that you are living in a prison of sin? The prison of sin could be defined as our human inability to be good, pure, righteous, kind, loving, holy, and sanctified. It is our inability to be obedient to the clear, revealed will of God. I got a letter a number of years ago from a lady who said,

> Steve, I'm leaving. I can't be good enough to continue with Christ. And I feel like such a hypocrite. I can't believe anymore. Because you believe, I know you won't understand, but I needed to tell you because I didn't want you to hate me. Please don't.

Sin separates you from yourself, from others, and from God. I get criticized a lot by people who say that I teach antinomianism—a lack of regard for God's moral law. Or that I teach *grace*—and that is too radical! They are afraid that some of those who hear or read my teachings on grace will say, "Good, I can sin all I want to sin, and it will be fun."

But let me tell you something: In all the years I have been walking with Christ, I have never met a Christian man or woman who didn't want to be better than he or she was. If you want to be better and can't be, then you—just like every other human being who has ever lived—are living in the prison of sin.

The second prison of what we do is *the prison of guilt.* David speaks in Psalm 32:1–2 as one who has been freed from his prison of guilt:

> Blessed is he whose transgression is forgiven,
> Whose sin is covered.
> Blessed is the man to whom the Lord does not impute iniquity,
> And in whose spirit there is no deceit.

Wouldn't it be nice to feel that way? The prison of guilt results from our failure to live either by (1) the standards of God, (2) what we believe to be the standards of God, or, (3) impossible standards we have created for ourselves. In their efforts to escape this prison, people usually either leave their faith or choose to live a lie.

There is real guilt, and there is false guilt. Real guilt is when you do something bad and feel properly guilty. False guilt is when you didn't do anything bad but still feel guilty. If you feel guilty every time a swarm of locusts attacks a Third World country, that is probably false guilt. Whether true or false, guilt can be quite debilitating.

Thirdly there is *the prison of failure.* Paul speaks in Philippians 4:13 as someone free from this kind of prison, when he says, "I can do all things through Christ who strengthens me." So does King Solomon, when he observes that "wisdom brings success" (Ecclesiastes 10:10).

What is the prison of failure? It is the neurotic sense Christians can often have that, because of their sin, they don't deserve success. That sense of unworthiness often creates failure in the Christian's life. You have heard that "God helps those who help themselves." That is a lie. God helps, and gives success to, those who can't help themselves and who know it. That is a key point of biblical teaching. There is a syllogism that most of us believe. Major premise: Christians are undeserving sinners. Minor premise: I am a Christian. Conclusion: I don't deserve success. Let me give you a better syllogism. Major premise: Christians are undeserving sinners. Minor premise: As a Christian, I am a sinner—but I am a *forgiven* sinner. Conclusion: I deserve success.

When Christians are failures it is usually for one of two reasons—either they are afraid to risk, or they feel that they don't deserve success. And let me tell you something: If you think you are a horrible sinner and don't deserve any success, you are living in a prison.

The Prisons of What We Think

Sin, guilt, and failure are the prisons we can put ourselves in by what we do. Next we come to the prisons that result from the way we think, and the first of these is *the prison of the past*. (By the way, you'll see that a number of these prisons overlap, but we have to define them separately in order to understand them.)

King David knew well how the past could be a prison:

Behold, I was brought forth in iniquity,
And in sin my mother conceived me. (Psalm 51:5)

The prison of the past has to do with dysfunctional family situations, resulting from past failures within the family. Most Christians carry enough baggage from their past to break the back of an elephant. The cumulative burden of your past and your parents' past is inversely proportional to how much you have appropriated God's grace.

I used to think the past didn't matter. I knew there were some sleeping dogs in my own past. My grandfather committed suicide. My father was an alcoholic. There were lots of dysfunctions in our family. But I decided I was going to let those sleeping dogs lie. When they finally woke up, they scared me to death! But they also helped explain some of the reasons I act the way I act in the present.

If you are from a bad family situation, and it affects your present, it is a prison.

The second prison of thought is *the prison of self-abasement*. This is what someone has called "wormology." In Romans 12:3 Paul says,

> For I say, through the grace given to me, to everyone who is among you, not to think of himself more highly than he ought to think, but to think soberly, as God has dealt to each one a measure of faith.

Wormologists are people who dwell on the first part of that verse, while ignoring the second part. The prison of self-abasement is characterized by "Humble Harry." We are in this prison if we constantly need to talk about how horrible we are and how little we deserve. The prison of self-abasement is the acceptance of what have been called the four adult human fears—rejection, failure, punishment, and shame—as a lifestyle that we deserve.

There is nothing worse, dear friend, than false humility. My friend and mentor Fred Smith talks about a woman who sang in a church, and he really liked what she sang. She was good, though not great. He went up to her and said, "Young lady, I sure did appreciate your singing."

She hung her head and said, "Oh, it isn't me, it is God's spirit."

And Fred said, "Well, I heard God's spirit do a whole lot better through Jerome Hines last week."

Humility doesn't mean wringing your hands and talking about how horrible you are. Humility is looking at yourself as you really are. As Paul says, it means looking at yourself "soberly," through the eyes of faith. Some Christians like to stand in a corner and say, "I'm only a worm." Well, if you do a lot of that sort of thing, then you are in the prison of self-abasement.

The sixth prison—the third in the "prisons of what we think" group—is *the prison of perfectionism*. Paul reminds us that, although we will someday be fully clothed in Christ's perfection, while we live on Planet Earth we only "know in part," "prophesy in part," and "see in a mirror, dimly" (1 Corinthians 13:9, 12). The prison of perfectionism is reflected in the need to achieve perfection in this life, or in the expectation of such perfection of other people. The prison of perfectionism is the prison of feeling that you don't have the right to be human.

Dear friend, we live in a fallen world. In this fallen world, if you get 51 percent you ought to file it under success. If you get 60, you're doing great. If you get 80 percent, you're something else. If you get 100 you're lying to yourself and to other people. My friend Israel Moses Kreps likes to say, "I have learned that there is only one messiah per universe, and I'm not it."

Do you ever feel that you have to be perfect? Or that your friends have to be perfect? Or that your family has to be perfect? Or that your church has to be perfect? If you ever feel that way, you are probably miserable. You know why? Because you are living in a prison of perfectionism.

The Prisons of How We Relate to Others

Next we come to the three prisons of how we relate to others. The first of these is *the prison of fear*. In 2 Timothy 1:7 we read that,

> God has not given us a spirit of fear, but of power and of love and of a sound mind.

The prison of fear is characterized by an undue feeling of distress about our circumstances. It is reflected in an inability to take risks. In my communications and homiletics classes at Reformed Theological Seminary, I like to teach the five points, or "tulip," of communication. The *u* of the tulip stands for *unconventional*. I say to the young men who are going into the ministry, "Look, the *u* stands for unconventional. That means, if you think you shouldn't say it, you probably should!"

I read an interesting quote the other day: "So risk your life on Christ, that if He has not told you the truth, you will have lost everything." Without taking anything away from that godly advice, let me put my own spin on it: So challenge the conventional that tradition-bound Christians will doubt your salvation.

Do you ever risk? Do you ever say what you really think? If you can never take a risk because you are afraid of what will happen to you, you are living in a prison, and it is called the prison of fear.

The second prison of how we relate to others is *the prison of needing approval*. Paul makes a bold statement in his first letter to the Corinthians:

> It is required in stewards that one be found faithful. But with me it is a very small thing that I should be judged by you. (1 Corinthians 4:2–3)

Have you ever said that? I hardly ever feel that way—that it doesn't matter what people think, that I'm responsible only to God. Quite the contrary, I am usually concerned about what others are thinking of me more than I'd care to admit.

What is the prison of needing approval? It is the need to always please everyone. It is characterized by basing one's identity on what people think rather than on what God has said in His Word. Christians spend an incredible amount of their time conforming themselves to whatever it takes to maintain their relationships of love with others. In fact, they'll even be "phoney" in order to maintain the approval of others. As Calvin Miller has written in *The Singer*, it is hard to keep on singing when the audience has turned its back.[2] If your "audience" is not God, but other people, then you are not going to sing very well; or you are only going to sing the songs they want you to sing.

Let me admit something to you: It is important to me that you like this book! You scare me to death! I want you to think highly of me. But I'll tell you something else: God scares me to death more than you do, and I want to please Him more than I want to please you. And that is why I trust that you will only read truth in this book.

If you are overly concerned with what other people think, then you are living in a prison. It is called the prison of needing approval.

Next comes *the prison of obligation.* This prison is characterized by the need to fix and rescue. It is the belief that every problem has a solution and that *you* are responsible for that solution. Martha, sister of Lazarus, tried to put Jesus into a prison of obligation:

Lord, if You had been here, my brother would not have died. (John 11:21)

But Jesus refused to be placed in that prison. He was faithful to the Father's plan for Lazarus, not to the obligation Martha tried to place on him.

I'll bet you didn't read your Bible today. I'll bet you haven't witnessed to anyone in over a month. I'll bet you have missed church recently. The way you are feeling when I say those things is the guilt that can cause you to feel an obligation to go out and fix everything that's wrong with the world.

The prison of obligation makes you a repairer and fixer of some things that God doesn't even want to fix. I talk with a lot of parents who are so worried about their children that they constantly try to "fix it." But God never acts until they quit trying to fix it.

Are you a fixer or rescuer? Then you are living in a prison. Only God is the real fixer and rescuer. Your prison is called the prison of obligation.

The Prisons of How Others Control Us

Finally we come to the last set of prisons, the prisons of how others control us. The first of these is *the prison of rules*. Paul knew some people caught in this prison:

> I marvel that you are turning away so soon from Him who called you in the grace of Christ, to a different gospel. (Galatians 1:6)

The "different gospel" was the attempt of some church leaders to convince Gentile Christians that their salvation depended on their also obeying the Law of Moses. The prison of rules is characterized by the spurious belief that the world runs by rules and that, if one can live by all the rules, everything will be fine. Jay Kesler once said that, "If being a Christian means obeying the rules, then the best Christian in my household is my dog." You see, we have this idea that there is this great pair of scales, with good on one side and bad on the other side . . . and we must try to keep the good outweighing the bad, by following the rules.

If you were nice, your mother said, then everything would be all right. Well, that is an old wives' tale even if your mother did say it. Paul Tournier said a *neurotic* is a person who can't say "damn" without the fear of losing his or her salvation. If you are constantly trying to live by the rules, then you are living in a prison.

Then there is *the prison of religion*. We learn from Amos 5:21–23 that God does not particularly care for empty religion:

> I hate, I despise your feast days,
> And I do not savor your sacred assemblies.
> Though you offer Me burnt offerings
>   and your grain offerings,
> I will not accept them,
> Nor will I regard your fattened peace offerings.
> Take away from Me the noise of your songs,
> For I will not hear
>   the melody of your stringed instruments.

Jesus expresses similar feelings in Matthew 23:15:

> Woe to you, scribes and Pharisees, hypocrites! For you travel land and sea to win one proselyte, and when he is won, you make him twice as much a son of hell as yourselves.

What is the prison of religion? It is the confusion of religious institutions with the reality of a relationship with God. And it is characterized by an undue involvement with and commitment to institutions. I don't know about you, but I am sick of religion. I prayed one time, "Lord, I'm so tired of it." And He said, "Child, I'm a little tired of it Myself."

There is a distinct difference between institutions and institutionalism. Institutions are necessary for us humans to accomplish anything worthwhile. If two or more people want to accomplish anything together, they must form an institution. *Institutionalism*, on the other hand, is when you keep on doing what you originally meant to do—but you don't know why anymore. Did you hear about the man whose job description was to tap on the wheels of trains? Someone asked him one day, "Why do you do that?" And he said, "I don't know, but I never miss one."

Why do you pray so much?

Why do you go to church so much?

Why do you allow yourself to say yes, yes, yes, so much when you ought to be saying no?

Don't get me wrong. Praying and going to church are good ideas. After all, they're God's ideas! But the question must still be asked: Are you in a prison of religion?

Finally, there is *the prison of gurus*: We tend to associate the word *guru* with the would-be holy men of Eastern religions, but even the Old Testament prophet Ezekiel had encountered his share of gurus:

> And the word of the LORD came to me, saying, "Son of man, prophesy against the prophets of Israel who prophesy, and say to those who prophesy out of their own heart, 'Hear the word of the LORD!'" Thus says the Lord GOD: "Woe to the foolish prophets, who follow their own spirit and have seen nothing!" (Ezekiel 13:1–3)

What is the prison of gurus? It is the belief that there are spiritual authority figures who have a special relationship with God and therefore deserve total, absolute submission. It is the suspicion that others know what is right or good for you better than *you* know what is right for yourself.

One time I missed a funeral. Well, I got there, but I was late. I thought it was to be in the afternoon but it was in the morning. I came screeching in about an hour late. The funeral director was standing in the parking lot and, seeing how anxious I was, said, "Just settle down, just be still. There are three people here today who can do no wrong: you, me, and the corpse."

It scares me that anyone would view this book as something given by a guru who knows better than they do. Look, I am not your mother. I am a beggar telling other beggars where I found bread. One time I was speaking for a conference where my friend, Ken Nanfelt, provided the singing. I said, "Ken, I'm not prepared. I guess I'm just going to have to trust God."

And he said, "Steve, it's awful that you have to trust God. God might fail you."

Then, when he saw my look of surprise at what he had said, he laughed and added, "If God fails anybody, it's going to be Billy Graham or the pope; He's not going to start with a peon like you!"

Your pastor, your Bible teacher, your favorite television teacher—all of those people put their pants or their skirts on just like you do. And they aren't any closer to God than you. We are in this thing together. When you start unduly submitting to authority figures, then you are in a prison of gurus.

Well, those are the prisons. In the next chapter we're going to try to figure out how so many Christians manage to become prisoners. Jesus says,

> Come to Me, all you who labor and are heavy laden, and I will give you rest. Take My yoke upon you and learn from Me, for I am gentle and lowly in heart, and you will find rest for your souls. For My yoke is easy and My burden is light. (Matthew 11:28–30)

Dear friend, that's not the Jesus of the gurus or the legalists, that is the Jesus of the Bible. He doesn't want you to be in any of those prisons we have looked at. Contrary to whatever you might have heard, His will is to set you free.

Nikita Khrushchev, former leader of the Soviet Union,

was once giving a speech about the difficulty and horrors Russians had endured under Joseph Stalin. A questioner in the crowd shouted, "Why didn't you speak out?"

Khrushchev's demeanor changed, his eyes flashed, and he became very angry and shouted, "Who said that?"

Nobody moved. You could have heard a pin drop. Then he started laughing and said, "That is why I didn't speak out!"

You weren't created for prison, and it is time you spoke out. It is scary, but on the other side of the prison door there is a wonderful freedom, and that is what this book is all about.

2

How and Why Christians Become Prisoners

In this chapter we're going to try to figure out how and why Christians become prisoners. Why would anyone who has responded to God's gift of salvation by grace, voluntarily confine himself or herself to any of those prisons we looked at in chapter 1—or to any of the many other prisons we haven't named?

David the psalmist shows us that mankind is intended for far more than living in prisons:

> When I consider Your heavens, the work of Your fingers,
> The moon and the stars, which You have ordained,
> What is man that You are mindful of him,
> And the son of man that You visit him?
> For You have made him a little lower than the angels,
> And You have crowned him with glory and honor.
>
> You have made him to have dominion
>   over all the works of Your hands.
> You have put all things under his feet,
> All sheep and oxen—
> Even the beasts of the field,
> The birds of the air,
> And the fish of the sea
> That pass through the paths of the seas.
>
> O Lord, our Lord,
> How excellent is Your name in all the earth! (Psalm 8:3–9)

What is man? What are we, individually, as men and women? We're going to start out with a study in biblical anthropology. Christians know very little about human nature, and most of the time they don't face the implications of what they do know. We are going to examine the truth about us prisoners—truth that isn't always pleasant, but is always true.

Two Ways of Looking at People

Let's begin by comparing the two basic anthropological views of mankind. This will lay the groundwork for everything else we consider. The first view says that *man is basically good, with a proclivity for evil.* The second view says that *man is basically evil, with a proclivity for good.* From what you know about human nature, which of those propositions do you accept?

Have you heard the story of the scorpion and the frog? They were standing on the side of a swollen river, and the scorpion said, "I sure would like to get across that river, and so would you, Mr. Frog. Can I ride on your back?"

The frog said, "Are you crazy! If you ride on my back, you will sting me and kill me."

The scorpion said, "Don't be silly. If I killed you, it would kill me too. We would both go down."

The frog said, "That makes sense, get on my back."

So they started across the river, and about halfway across, the scorpion stung the frog. Just as they were going down for the final time, the frog said, "I knew it! I knew you would sting me!"

And the scorpion said, "I didn't really mean to—it's just my nature."

The moral of the story? Before you do business with a scorpion, make sure you know something about "scorpion nature."

You have to do the same thing with human nature. If mankind is basically good, then we should remove all our man-made social institutions so that all the basic goodness will be able to come out. In terms of educational philosophy, we should get out of the kids' way and let them learn naturally—because they are basically good.

While we're at it, we'll need to get rid of all militaristic leaders.

We'll get rid of anything that could cause poverty, because once people have enough money we'll be able to eliminate all greed.

We'll give everyone the opportunity to do whatever they want to do, thereby eliminating selfish ambition.

We'll trust totally in the ability of our government to take all of us noble savages and provide us a perfectly just society . . . and we'll no longer be savages!

The Bible takes the second view—that *man is basically evil, but with a proclivity for good.* This is the clear message of Psalm 14:

> They are corrupt,
> They have done abominable works,
> There is none who does good.
>
> The LORD looks down from heaven
>   upon the children of men,
> To see if there are any who understand, who seek God.
> They have all turned aside.
> They have together become corrupt;
> There is none who does good,
> No, not one. (verses 1–3)

I know this assessment of mankind sounds unpleasant, but stay with me, because we are going to build on this something that will change your life. But first, we might as well pile on some more unpleasantness:

> The heart is deceitful above all things,
> And desperately wicked;
> Who can know it? (Jeremiah 17:9)

> If we say that we have not sinned, we make Him a liar, and
> His word is not in us. (1 John 1:10)

If, as the Bible says, man is basically evil with a proclivity
for good (remember Psalm 8!), it explains a whole lot of stuff,
doesn't it? It explains war. It explains why in all of written
human history, there have been only three years of peace. It
explains why "values clarification" classes in high schools
simply don't work. I have talked to teachers who didn't
believe in God who had thought that values clarification
would work. Having tried it, they said to me, "Steve, this is a
waste of time."

If mankind is basically evil, it explains why government
is so sick. It explains why "power corrupts, and absolute
power corrupts absolutely." It explains why advertisements
lie to you. Why greed is so rampant. It explains sexual
harassment. It explains why you're always tempted to cheat
on your income tax return.

It explains why any Christian who understands biblical
anthropology ought to lock his or her car!

Man's basic evil nature is also one of the main reasons
you and I are in our prisons. When you became a Christian,
you became basically good—right? Wrong, wrong, wrong!
Look at what the apostle Paul says about himself in Romans
7. Remember that this was written by the man who wrote
much of the New Testament, who was the first Christian
missionary. If ever anyone was sanctified and good, with
only a slight proclivity for evil, it was Paul. But listen to what
he says:

> We know that the law is spiritual, but I am carnal, sold under
> sin. For what I am doing, I do not understand. For what I will
> to do, that I do not practice; but what I hate, that I do. . . . For I
> know that in me (that is, in my flesh) nothing good dwells; for
> to will is present with me, but how to perform what is good I
> do not find. For the good that I will to do, I do not do; but the

evil that I will not to do, that I practice. (Romans 7:14–15, 18–19)

Becoming a Christian enabled you to label sin properly, and it made you sensitive to sin. A little boy once said that becoming a Christian "didn't stop me from sinning, but it sure took the fun out of it!" Becoming a Christian gave you forgiveness when you sinned; and it gave you the power to become a little bit better every day. But becoming a Christian did not eliminate your sinful nature.

I used to think that there were two kinds of people in this world—the good ones and the bad ones. The good ones were in church and the bad ones weren't. The good ones didn't mow their lawns on Sunday, while the bad ones mowed their lawns right outside the church window during the worship service. The good ones didn't smoke or drink too much, and the bad ones did all that stuff to excess. Well, I hadn't been a pastor for more than two weeks before I realized that I had been right about there being two kinds of people . . . I had just made a mistake about who they were: There are the bad people who *know* they are bad, and bad people who don't know it.

We Don't Realize Why We're So Bad

Remember, the question before the house is, Why are we, as redeemed children of God, living in these various kinds of prisons? Now that we have examined the two opposing views of human nature, I'm going to give you the first reason for our imprisonment. We are still in prison because *we don't understand the source of evil and sin.* Let's look at *two people* whom we meet very early in the pages of Scripture. In fact, they're the first people we meet—Adam and Eve:

Nevertheless death reigned from Adam to Moses, even over those who had not sinned according to the likeness of the transgression of Adam, who is a type of Him who was to come. (Romans 5:14)

For since by man came death . . . (1 Corinthians 15:21)

For as in Adam all die . . .(verse 22)

Long before you were born, two people did some bad stuff and it affected you and it really isn't fair. You don't really understand biblical anthropology until you understand what theologians call the Fall. The famed financier and statesman Bernard Baruch, when appearing before a Senate hearing, was asked how to prevent the periodic ups and downs in our nation's economy. He said, "I know how to do it. Pass a law changing human nature. Make it retroactive to the Garden of Eden."

Perhaps you've heard the poem about the three monkeys discussing evolution:

> Listen, you two,
> It can't be true,
> There's a rumor going 'round
> That's a very ill sound,
> That man descended from our noble race.
> Why, the very idea is a dire disgrace!
> You'll never see
> 'Round the coconut tree
> A monkey fence—
> It doesn't make sense.
> And then let the coconuts go to waste,
> Forbidding other monkeys to have a taste.
> Here's another thing a monkey won't do:
> Go out at night and get on a stew,
> Or use a gun or a knife
> To take another monkey's life.
> Yes, man descended, that ordinary cuss,
> But, brothers, he didn't descend from us.

No, we certainly didn't! It all started with our human

parents, Adam and Eve. Long before you or I were born, our first mother and father did some bad things in disobedience to God, and introduced something abnormal into human nature. So one of the reasons we are in a prison is because it is our natural proclivity to climb into one.

Here's an important principle that we'll come back to later on: Adamic sin is repeated and, without God's grace, it is magnified in every generation within family lines. The Bible says it over and over again. Let me give you just one text:

> For I, the LORD your God, am a jealous God, visiting the iniquity of the fathers upon the children to the third and fourth generations of those who hate Me, but showing mercy to thousands, to those who love Me, and keep My commandments. (Exodus 20:5–6)

You say, "Steve, that's not fair."

You're right, it's not fair. I'm not telling you stuff that is fair, I'm telling you stuff that is true, and I'm giving you some facts. My grandfather committed suicide, my father was an alcoholic, and I have everything that caused my grandfather's suicide and my father's alcoholism in me. It's in me, and I have it in double portion. But God has shown me His love and forgiveness and grace. And He has broken the cycle of generationally-repeated sin in those particular areas.

Adamic sin is repeated, and without God's grace it is magnified in every generation within family lines.

We Don't Realize How Good We Can Be

We can live in a prison because we don't realize why we tend to do the wrong thing. Ironically, we also can become confined to a prison because of not realizing how good we can be. We don't understand that, even though we are born

as sinners, *as Christians we also have a great potential for good.*
To understand why we're bad, we have only to look at two
people—Adam and Eve. To understand our proclivity to be
good in spite of our sinful nature inherited from those two
people, we'll take a look at *two attractions.*

Remember that, according to biblical anthropology, we
humans have an inborn evil nature, but we also have a
proclivity for good. It stands to reason, of course, that these
two parts of our human nature will be in conflict with each
other. Paul tells us very honestly how he experienced this
conflict in his own life:

> For I delight in the law of God according to the inward man.
> But I see another law in my members, warring against the law
> of my mind, and bringing me into captivity to the law of sin
> which is in my members. O wretched man that I am! Who will
> deliver me from this body of death? (Romans 7:22–24)

In other words, there is a struggle going on. There's an
interesting story about an eagle egg that mistakenly was
hatched by a chicken. The eagle really looked funny, trying to
peck around like a chicken. He always felt that he was
different. To be quite honest, he didn't even like corn. He saw
that he was bigger than his brothers and sisters, and he never
felt at home. Then one day, in the distance, there was a spot
moving across the sky, and as it came closer, it became clear
that it was an eagle. And then there was the eagle cry. And
the young eagle heard the cry, stretched his wings, and
began to fly.

You know, Joe Pagan and Jane Cynic like that story, but it
doesn't really relate to them. It is not a story for pagans. You
know why? Because they don't get any choice. Before you
knew Christ, did you sometimes think you were different?
Before you found Him, did you ever say to yourself, *I'm made
for something better than this*?

Let me ask you something else: After you became a
Christian, did you feel that you had come to something new?

Did it feel like you were coming home? I have asked hundreds of Christians those questions, and they usually say something like, "Yeah, man, I used to think, *You know, I'm made for something better than this.* And when I became a Christian, of course, it was something new, but I did feel like I was coming home."

When you became a Christian, you were given the heart of an eagle. And the eagle and the chicken will always be in a fight. So get used to it. Don't be surprised when you desire to sin, when you desire to be disobedient. Don't be surprised either when you desire to be faithful and obedient.

We Don't Realize How Free We Can Be

The third reason we get locked up in our prisons is that *we don't understand that we can truly be free.* To understand this truth we'll take a look at *two alternatives.* As we have noted, Paul saw very clearly those two alternatives, those two opposing possibilities, in his own life:

> For I delight in the law of God. . . . But I see another law in my members . . .

Did you hear about the man who cut his hand very badly? They rushed him to the doctor, who performed emergency surgery. When it was all over, the man said, "Doc, will I be able to play the piano now?"

The doctor said, "Of course you can."

And the man replied, "That's wonderful! Because I never could play the piano before!"

Well, when you became a Christian, you were given the possibility of freedom. Before, you had only one alternative, and that was the prison. I get invited a lot of times to do motivational speaking for secular organizations. Once I was invited to do it for a group of banks. The money is really good for this kind of speaking, but I don't do it. You know why I don't do it? There are two reasons: First, I belong to the King, and it is hard not to talk about Him. Secondly, I turn those invitations down because giving a motivational speech to a pagan is sort of like giving a brand new dress to a man. He may like it, but it isn't going to do him any good. The pagan has only one alternative—the prison.

We Don't Realize How Royal We Are

The fourth reason we become prisoners is that *we don't realize that we are children of the King*. We have looked at the two people, the two attractions, and the two alternatives; to explore this final point we'll consider the *two positions*. Paul speaks of these two very different positions in Galatians 4:7:

> Therefore you are no longer a slave but a son, and if a son, then an heir of God through Christ.

Many of us Christians suffer from a horrible inferiority complex. We see ourselves as a child of a slave rather than the child of the King. Someone told me a story that was told about Fred Craddock, an author and seminary professor. Craddock and his wife were up in the mountains of Tennessee at one of those lookout places. An old man came over to the Craddocks and started talking to them. After a while he asked, "Well, Fred, what is it that you do?"

Craddock said, "I'm a homiletics professor."

The old man said, "Preacher, huh? Well, I have a good story to tell you." Then he put his arm around Craddock and said, "My name is Ben Hooper. I grew up in a small town as a illegitimate son. Nobody knew who my father was. It was a horrible place to grow up. I can't tell you the shame I felt. It was far more shame than we know today. Today, you can be who you want to be, but in those days, if you didn't have a father, and your mother wasn't married, then you got into some serious, awful problems. So I grew up angry, and everybody in the town would always say, 'You know he looks like . . .' , and they would speculate about who my father was."

The old man continued, "There was a preacher in my town, and I liked him a lot because he didn't talk any nonsense. Sometimes I would slip into the back of the church and listen to his sermon because he said good things and I was attracted to him. But I would always leave as soon as the sermon was over, so that no one would stop me.

"One day I was a little late in getting out the back door of the church, and I felt a big hand on my shoulder. I turned around and it was the preacher. He said, 'Son, what is your name?' And I said, 'Ben Hooper, sir.' And then the preacher looked at me kind of quizzically, and he said, 'You know you look like . . .' , and he paused, and I thought, 'Not again!' But then he continued, 'Son, you look like the child of the King. Now go out and live like it.'"

Craddock said that when he got back to the car and started thinking about what the old man had told him, he kept saying the man's name over and over in his mind: *Ben Hooper . . . I've heard that name . . . Ben Hooper . . .*

Then he remembered! He remembered, as a child, hearing his father talk about a multi-term governor of Tennessee whose name was Ben Hooper . . . who had been an illegitimate son!

You too were once illegitimate. But now you are a part of the family, and freedom is yours. This book is going to teach you how to go out and live like who you are—a child of the King.

3

Why Christians Stay in Prison

In this chapter we are going to be asking, Once Christians get into their prisons, why do so many of them stay there so long? Let me give you a couple of verses:

As a dog returns to his own vomit,
So a fool repeats his folly. (Proverbs 26:11)

I marvel that you are turning away so soon from Him who called you in the grace of Christ, to a different gospel. (Galatians 1:6)

It always puzzles me that Christians want to stay in their prisons. If you read this book carefully, you'll realize that, though I may say it differently, I am simply teaching basic Bible doctrine—things that Christians have known all of their lives, if they have been in a church where the Bible was taught. I am not going to be saying radical things. None of this stuff is new. It is classic orthodox theology.

If that is true, and it is, why are Christians still in their prisons—if they have the road map to get out?

People are funny, and people are my business. Anyone who tells you that they understand people will lie about other things, too! One of my favorite chapters in the Bible is the eighth chapter of Exodus. You remember, God was inflicting a number of plagues on Pharaoh and the Egyptians, in order to force them to set the Israelites free. A plague would come. Pharaoh would promise to let the people go. Then he would change his mind. Again and again. In verse 3 of Exodus 8, Moses inflicts on Egypt a plague of frogs. The frogs come, and very shortly, as he has done before, Pharaoh calls for Moses and says, "I've had enough." And once again he promises to let the Israelites go.

Then, in verse 9, Moses asks Pharaoh *how soon* he would like the frogs to leave! And incredibly, Pharaoh says, "Do it tomorrow"!

I don't understand that. I don't understand people—just like Paul didn't understand the believers in Galatia. "I marvel . . . ," or, in contemporary language, "I'm really surprised that you guys are turning away so soon from Him who called you in the grace of Christ, to a different gospel." People who are free, rejecting their freedom? It was amazing to Paul and it is amazing to me.

The prisons I have described to you are not necessary. Over the next few chapters, I'm going to be giving you some very exciting news about how to get out of those prisons. But to be honest with you, some of you are going to decide to stay in your prisons anyway. The question before the house is, Why?

Some People Want to Keep Us There!

Sometimes we find ourselves staying in our prisons of sin and failure and fear and rules because there are people who want to keep us there. I call such people the *keepers* of the cell. Paul knew all about the cell-keepers in the church at Galatia:

> O foolish Galatians! *Who has bewitched you* that you should not obey the truth, before whose eyes Jesus Christ was clearly portrayed among you as crucified. (Galatians 3:1, emphasis added)

Paul was angry because the Judaizers had come in and "bewitched" the young Galatian believers back into a prison of legalism.

Sometimes I get angry too. Sometimes I get really ticked. I had a friend named Ron Henley. He was the founder of *The Dolphin Digest* magazine. He died in his thirties of cancer, and he found Christ just before he died. I spent many hours with Ron before he died in that hospital room. And I, as a pastor should do, prepared him for death. It was clear that, short of some kind of major miracle, God was not going to intervene at that point. He was going to call Ron home. So I read the Scriptures, and prepared Ron for death.

I came in one day and Ron was upset, afraid, angry, and mean. He was yelling at everyone. I got everyone out of the room and asked Ron what was wrong. He said, "I found out that my cancer comes from demons."

I said, "Who told you that?" And he named a man who was well-known as an exorcist. This exorcist had come into Ron's room the night before and performed an exorcism ceremony. He said the reason Ron had cancer was because his wife had a book on numerology in the library. Ron's parents, who were not Christians at the time, were absolutely devastated. They didn't know what was going on.

Let me tell you something: I got really ticked at that guy. I called him and said some very unpastoral things. I said, "If you ever again visit anybody in the church where I am the pastor without my permission, I want you to know, I am coming after you."

That man had taken Ron, who had been freed to die, and had put him in a prison. I always get angry when some neurotic Christian robs another Christian of his or her freedom. Paul tells us,

> But even if we, or an angel from heaven, preach any other gospel to you than what we have preached to you, let him be accursed. As we have said before, so now I say again, if anyone preaches any other gospel to you than what you have received, let him be accursed. (Galatians 1:8–9)

Some people stay in prison because the prison keepers have told them that it is "more spiritual" to be there. Be on the lookout for those keepers of the cell.

Prisons Are Secure

Second, Christians choose to stay in prison because of the *security* of the cell. In Exodus 14, God's people have made it to the Red Sea and are close to freedom. They look at the sea and realize there's no way they can get across . . . and Pharaoh's armies are closing in behind them. So they begin complaining to Moses. This is how the text reads:

> Because there were no graves in Egypt, have you taken us away to die in the wilderness? Why have you so dealt with us, to bring us up out of Egypt? Is this not the word we told you in Egypt, saying, "Let us alone that we may serve the Egyptians"? For it would have been better for us to serve the Egyptians than that we should die in the wilderness. (verses 11–12)

Faced with the dangers involved in claiming their freedom, those Israelites longed for the security of being slaves! If people get to choose between being a slave and being totally free—if people get to choose between totalitarianism and anarchy—they will choose totalitarianism every time. If you give people the choice of living under a dictator who controls every move they make, and living in total anarchy, they will choose the dictator every time. Security is more important to most people than freedom.

A pastor friend of mine became involved in a cult. He called me one night in tears and said, "Steve, I need some help, and you are my brother, and I am calling out to you. I've got to get out of this. I'm so bound. It's so legalistic. I want to be free again the way we were when we were friends. Would you help me?"

I said, "Sure."

He said, "Would you see if you could find a church that I could serve?"

I began to look, and three weeks later I found out that he had gone back into the cult. I thought, *Lord, why?*

I will tell you why: because of his need for the false security the cult provided. It feels safe to look and act and think the way others do. There is a certain comfort in being controlled by other people. Obeying the rules provides a kind of security. Don't forget about the false security of the cell.

Some People Enjoy Being Punished

Some people stay in the prison even after they know the truth of freedom, not only because of the keepers of the cell, or the security of the cell, but because it feels right to them to be punished. They actually enjoy the *punishment* of the cell.

Sometimes Christians needlessly submit to punishment because of faulty doctrine. Premise: "All have sinned and fall short of the glory of God" (Romans 3:23). Conclusion: All will be punished. Now, we are going to look into this a lot more later on. At this point, it is important that you see the syndrome. You say, "I'm no good." And you are right: You *are* no good. But you are valuable and loved by the God of the universe, and He is going to make you like Jesus.

You're no good, and I'm no good, so we stay in a prison because we think we deserve the prison. If you think you are deserving of punishment, you will accept punishment. You say, "I like to pay my way. I'll take what's coming to me." So you stay in prison, to "do your time." You don't want to be "one down" on God.

A number of years ago, I talked with a man who accepted every bit of verbal abuse given to him by his coworkers and family . . . and there was a lot of it. I told him that, even if he was rarely a good person or rarely right, he had to be right and good at least some of the time.

He said, "Steve, if I'm a horrible sinner, there is nothing that could be said about me that isn't either true or potentially true."

"No," I replied, "you are a liar. Sometimes the things you do and say are right and proper, and when you don't recognize that or when you accept what others say when it isn't true, you have violated God's law about being truthful."

He said, "You're right."

It was then that I knew I wouldn't be able to help him. By calling him a liar, I had simply added one more item to his long list of sin and failure.

Prisons Are Safe

A lot of people stay in the prison cell even after they know how to get out—not only because of the keepers of the cell and the security of the cell and the punishment of the cell—some people stay there because of the *safety* in the cell. In John chapter 5, we find Jesus offering to heal a man who has been crippled for thirty-eight years. The text reads this way:

> When Jesus saw him lying there, and knew that he already had been in that condition a long time, He said to him, "Do you want to be made well?" (John 5:6)

If I had been the crippled man, I would have said, "Are you crazy? Do you think I *like* this! Thirty-eight years of this?"

But I have learned—and you have probably learned it too—that there is safety in being sick. No one expects much of you. You don't have to wash the dishes. You don't have to succeed. You don't have to risk. Because, after all, you are sick. Prison is like that. Prison can be a safe place. As we go on in this book I'm going to be asking you to risk in some pretty big ways. Freedom can be a pretty scary thing. Risk means that people might reject you. That you might get hurt. That you might be in pain. But without that risk you will stay in your prison cell.

As a young man, I had a friend whose mother was always afraid for him. She wouldn't let him have a bicycle because she was afraid he was going to get hurt. Wouldn't let him have any friends because we would be a bad influence on him. Sent him to a private Christian school, and then picked him up every day and wouldn't let him associate with anyone. When it came time for him to get a driver's license, she wouldn't let him have one because he might have an accident. Needless to say, he ended up rather neurotic. He is afraid to talk. He is afraid to reach out. He is afraid to risk just about anything.

That's the way "Mother Church" can be sometimes. We build a place that is militarily defensible, and we stay in the safety of the cell.

Prisons Give You a Sense of Control

Finally, some people stay in their prison cells, even when they know how to get out, because there is a sense of *control* in the cell. I am a teetotaler. I love to preach sermons against booze, because that is perhaps the only sin I don't have. I don't even like the stuff. To be honest with you, even though it always looks good, wine tastes to me like Kool-Aid gone bad. I was on a plane one time and they were serving free champagne. It was a good while until dinner and I thought, *Shoot! That looks so cold and bubbly and nice.* So I let them give me a glass of champagne. I took a sip of it and it tasted like medicine. It was awful. I was sitting there and it was a long time until dinner and I didn't want to hold this glass forever. So I did what you do with medicine. I chugged the stuff!

You guessed it! I got a buzz. I felt really nauseous, too. But I really didn't want to get up and go back to the bathroom, because I was afraid someone would see me weaving and wobbling—someone who listened to my "Key Life" radio show or had attended my seminars. And then, I imagined, the story would spread around that Steve Brown was an alcoholic.

I remembered someone telling me that if you ate something after drinking you would feel better. I bowed my head and said, "Lord, I won't ever do this again if, after eating something, I feel better." So I ate something, and it worked.

I don't like the taste of alcohol, but a more important reason that I don't drink is that I fear losing control. I fear that all the bad stuff in me would come out. I want to control things. Prison cells are small. You can control what goes on in them. Freedom is as big as God. Freedom can mean losing control of your little world—and that is pretty scary.

Some Christians are afraid to think, because they might think a bad thought.

We are told, "Don't risk; you might get into trouble." So Christians don't risk.

We are told, "Don't talk; you might say a cuss word; you might say the wrong thing." So we don't talk very much, except about "spiritual" things.

We are told, "Don't question, because you might find that some of the things you believed aren't true." So we never question.

We are told, "Don't break any rules, or you might get punished." So we live by rules.

Why do people stay in their prison cells?

Because not having to be responsible—letting the prison *keepers* do it all for you—is more important to most people than freedom.

Because false *security* is more important to most people than freedom.

Because most people prefer "taking their *punishment*" to being free.

Because *safety* is more important to most people than freedom.

Because being in *control* is more important to most people than freedom.

It makes me angry to see Christians going through life that way—maintaining perfect control . . . in their tiny little cells. It's almost as if an unborn child were to say, "I'm not going out there. It's too scary. I mean, I could get hurt out there. It can get cold sometimes. I think I'll just stay here where it is nice and warm."

Listen to me, dear friends: Some people stay in the Christian womb, never knowing love, risk, joy, or freedom—because it is warm.

Until they die. And then they find out they never lived.

4

Lies That Lock the Prison Doors

Now we're going to take a look at "the big D"—*denial*. It is the key concept in this entire book. You can violate almost anything I have been teaching, and still be free, as long as you are honest with yourself and honest before God—and, insofar as you need to be, open and honest before others.

If you want a renewed sense of spiritual power in your life, this chapter is the road. Let me show you some dangerous kinds of denial—lies that will kill your freedom, rob you of power, and keep you in prison.

"I'm Not in Any Pain"

Lie number one: *I'm not in prison, and there is no pain.* That kind of denial brings to mind the words of our Lord to the church of Laodicea:

> Because you say, "I am rich, have become wealthy, and have need of nothing"—and do not know that you are wretched, miserable, poor, blind, and naked—I counsel you to buy from Me gold refined in the fire, that you may be rich; and white garments, that you may be clothed, that the shame of your nakedness may not be revealed; and anoint your eyes with eye salve, that you may see. (Revelation 3:17–18)

Do you remember the story of Jesus healing the man born blind, in John chapter 9? The whole episode presented a problem for the religious authorities, who didn't want to admit that Jesus had performed a miracle. They questioned the parents, and tried to "break" the man's story. They huffed and they puffed. Then in verse 28 we read,

> Then they reviled him and said, "You are His disciple, but we are Moses' disciples."

Then the formerly blind man defended Jesus, and the religious authorities responded,

> "You were completely born in sins, and are you teaching us?" And they cast him out. (verse 34)

Do you see it? The religious leaders were saying, "We are pure and spiritual and kind and good and nice, and you are a sinner; and you are trying to teach us! You are trying to tell us that you were healed!"

Do you see it? Jesus the Son of God had come with power and grace and love, yet they were in such a state of denial that the only thing they could do was reject the plain evidence before them. Every time they saw that blind man walking around without a white cane, they were convicted and had to go into denial again.

When someone from Dayton, Ohio, heard that the Wright Brothers, who were from Dayton, had finally flown at Kitty Hawk, North Carolina, he was heard to mutter, "I don't believe it. I just don't believe it. Nobody is ever going to fly, and if anyone ever does, it won't be anyone from Dayton, Ohio."

One thing worse than being wretched and miserable and poor and blind and naked, is to be wretched and miserable and poor and blind and naked and not *know* that you are wretched and miserable and poor and blind and naked. In the words of Paul, "Let him who thinks he stands take heed lest he fall" (1 Corinthians 10:12).

In Bluefield, West Virginia, a number of years ago, I met a man named Bud. He took me out to dinner at a steak house. As we sat down, he pointed out the window and said, "Do you see that mountain up there?"

I said that I did.

He said, "When I first became a Christian, I went throughout the city telling pastors what they ought to know, and telling my brothers and sisters what they ought to know. They weren't ready to be corrected, so I went up on that mountain and looked out over my town and said, 'Lord, I'm the only one left.'"

"What did the Lord say?" I asked him.

He replied, "The Lord said, 'You've got to be kidding!'"

The only people Christ didn't help were those who thought that they didn't need help.

I know there are problems with Alcoholics Anonymous, but I love AA. They are a good bunch of people doing a great work. And the best thing about AA is that those folks are honest. When they introduce themselves at an AA meeting, they say, "Hi! I'm Joe, and I'm an alcoholic." We ought to adopt that kind of honesty in the church. We should say, "Hi, I'm Sara, and I'm the church gossip." "Hi, I'm Bill, and I'm an adulterer." "Hi, I'm Jane, and I'm scared of living." "Hi, I'm Jack, and I'm thinking about suicide." "Hi, I'm George, and I'm gay."

God only fights battles with wounded soldiers. The doctrine of radical and pervasive depravity is an important doctrine and it is taught throughout Scripture. Fred Smith loves to go around asking people, "If you were arrested for drunken driving on Saturday night and it was in the paper on Sunday morning, would you go to church?"

I have seen him ask a lot of people that. Most people say, "Well, I think I'd let it die down for a few weeks before I went back to church."

(When he asked me, I was a pastor and I said, "No, I

wouldn't go to church—because I wouldn't have a job!")

When people respond that way to Fred's question, he always laughs and says, "You know, that's silly. That's just as if a man had been hit by an automobile and his ribs were broken, and his clothes torn, and they come in the ambulance to take him to the hospital . . . and just as they are getting ready to pick up the stretcher, he says, 'Guys, wait just a second! I look horrible! Let me go home and tape up these ribs, wash up a little bit, put on a new suit—*then* I'll come to the hospital!'"

The church is a hospital for sinners. And the one place you ought to be when you have sinned is in church. But we don't do it that way. Now, you're probably not reading this book unless you're tired of playing those kinds of games. Well, I'm tired of playing those games too. People who say they have no pain and are not in prison never get out. "Those who are well have no need of a physician, but those who are sick. I have not come to call the righteous, but sinners, to repentance" (Luke 5:31–32).

If you are not a sinner, then you don't have any need for Jesus. If you are not unqualified, if you are not in prison, if you are not in pain, then the Christian faith simply is not for you.

That is the first lie that can keep us locked up: I'm not in prison, and there really is no pain.

"I Must Accept It"

The second lie is, *I must accept the prison and the pain.* Do you remember this story from the book of Acts:

> Now Peter and John went up together to the temple at the hour of prayer, the ninth hour. And a certain man lame from his mother's womb was carried, whom they laid daily at the gate of the temple which is called Beautiful, to ask alms from those who entered the temple; who, seeing Peter and John about to go into the temple, asked for alms. And fixing his

eyes on him, with John, Peter said, "Look at us." So he gave them his attention, expecting to receive something from them. Then Peter said, "Silver and gold I do not have, but what I do have I give you: In the name of Jesus Christ of Nazareth, rise up and walk." And he took him by the right hand and lifted him up, and immediately his feet and ankle bones received strength. So he, leaping up, stood and walked and entered the temple with them—walking, leaping and praising God. And all the people saw him walking and praising God. Then they knew that it was he who sat begging alms at the Beautiful Gate of the temple; and they were filled with wonder and amazement at what had happened to him. (Acts 3:1–10)

I'm a cynic. My philosophy is that you are born in one hospital and you die in another, and the meaning of life is to get from the one hospital to the other without screwing up too bad.

That isn't true, of course. My problem is that sometimes I just deal with life in a stoical way. And sometimes that falls over into my teaching for a number of months. For awhile during my years as a pastor, I taught that prosperity theology—the idea that you can be wealthy and healthy and all that stuff if you exercise the proper principles—was simply a lie. And I said it so often that I got the people to believe that God didn't answer prayers. Now, I didn't do that on purpose. But that was the practical result of what I said.

Then we started having healing services. That's right— healing services in a Presbyterian church! We had them once every quarter, with the elders anointing people with oil. It was a moving experience and God answered some wondrous prayers in some amazing and miraculous ways.

Let me tell you something: The first thing I had to do was get that congregation to believe that God answered prayers—after I had unloaded all my cynicism on them. Now, you may have begun reading this book thinking, *I've always been this way. It's hard, but by God's grace, I will accept it.*

That is noble, but it is a lie. You don't have to be guilty all the time. You don't have to be manipulated or afraid all the time. The prison and the pain don't have to be accepted. Just say, "I'm not going to accept it anymore."

A little later on, I'm going to show you some ways to do that.

"I Deserve the Pain"

Lie number three: *I deserve the prison and the pain.* How does that statement stack up in light of these truths from Scripture:

> There is therefore now no condemnation to those who are in Christ Jesus, who do not walk according to the flesh, but according to the Spirit. For the law of the Spirit of life in Christ Jesus has made me free from the law of sin and death. (Romans 8:1)

> For you did not receive the spirit of bondage again to fear, but you received the Spirit of adoption by whom we cry out, "Abba, Father." (verse 15)

You deserve the prison and the pain? Of course you do. So do I. But Jesus doesn't! And you are in Him. He is your elder brother. And because Jesus is your elder brother, you deserve royal treatment.

The Civil War was still raging and one young soldier had already lost his father and both of his brothers in the conflict. His mother was getting ready for harvest time at their farm, and the boy wanted to go home to help her, fearing that otherwise they would go bankrupt.

He went to his sergeant, and the sergeant said, "Son, it sounds good to me, but I think you need to go to Washington and ask the commander-in-chief."

So the young man was given leave by the sergeant to go to Washington. Just as he was starting up the steps of the White House, a guard stopped him and said, "What do you want?"

He told him the story.

The guard said, "Look, young man, go back to your unit. You are a soldier, not a farmer. Go back and fight the way you are supposed to fight."

As you can imagine, the young soldier was absolutely devastated. He knew that his widowed, bereaved mother wouldn't be able to harvest the crops, and that the farm would be lost.

A little later, as he was walking through the streets of Washington, a little boy came up to him and said, "Mister, you look horrible! Can I help you?"

The young man thought to himself, *What can it hurt? I need to tell someone; and I'll never see this kid again.*

So he just told him the story.

When he had finished pouring out all the pain, the little boy said, "I think I can help." He took the soldier by the hand and said, "Come with me." He led him through the streets of Washington and right up to the White House, past the guard, up the stairs, into the office of the president of the United States—and Abraham Lincoln looked up and said, "Yes, Tad, what do you want."

Because that little boy happened to be the president's son, the soldier's request was granted. We have something better than that. According to Hebrews 7:25 you and I are on the prayer list of Jesus Himself:

> . . . He always lives to make intercession for them.

Jesus is continually talking to the Father about you and me.

All of my life as a pastor, I wanted a big church. I mean one of those mega-churches that look sort of like a city. I wanted to be the pastor of the First Mega-church on the corner of First and Main. It never happened. Don't get me wrong, I'm where I'm supposed to be. God took the bad stuff and was sovereign, and used it to get me to do what I'm doing. But there were a number of times when I was offered very large churches. I turned them down, and do you know why? Because I didn't think I deserved them.

Some of you ought to be doing far better than you are right now. Do you ever wonder why, when you get close to success, you always blow it? Because of Christ, you deserve anything God grants you. I'm not talking just about success. I'm talking about relationships. I'm talking about being a bold Christian.

The reason we are wimps is because we don't think we deserve anything better than the worst. When my wife, Anna, and I were young, in college, and dating, I worked for a laundry and made twenty-five cents a shirt. I barely got by. Some of the other guys took their girlfriends to dinner and the theater. I didn't have that kind of money and I said to Anna, "I wish I had the money to go to the theater with you, and to do those kinds of things."

She said to me then what she has said to me many times since then: "Steve, I don't care where we go as long as I'm with you."

You know, we ought to say that to the Father. "Father, I don't care where we go, as long as I'm with You."

And do you know what? The Father won't always lead you to things you don't want to do and places where you don't want to be. The Father desires to say yes to you. He desires to see you successful. He desires to see you raised up in the eyes of people so that you can point to Him. The Father says, "I have a lot of power and freedom and love to spend on you, if you would only accept it."

"I Can't Get Out of Here!"

Lie number four is, *I can't change the prison and the pain.* In Matthew 16:18, Peter has just given his great confession about Jesus being the Christ, the Son of the living God, and Jesus says to him,

And I also say to you that you are Peter, and on this rock I will build My church, and the gates of Hades shall not prevail against it.

I used to think that we as the church sort of had this gate, and Satan and his demons couldn't get in. But have you ever been attacked by a gate? Jesus is saying *we* are to go on the attack. *We* are to break down the gates of hell—and the gates of hell will not be able to prevail against us:

Then the seventy returned with joy, saying, "Lord, even the demons are subject to us in Your name." (Luke 10:17)

For though we walk in the flesh, we do not war according to the flesh. For the weapons of our warfare are not carnal but mighty in God for pulling down strongholds. (2 Corinthians 10:3–4)

Those verses say unmistakably that we *can* change our imprisoned situation.

But why, if all this is true, do Christians still feel guilty and lack freedom and power? Why? Because there are supernatural powers that have a vested interest in keeping you in your prison:

Put on the whole armor of God, that you may be able to stand against the wiles of the devil. For we do not wrestle against flesh and blood, but against principalities, against powers, against the rulers of the darkness of this age, against spiritual hosts of wickedness in the heavenly places. (Ephesians 6:11–12)

Back in the early days, when I didn't know Christ but was still a pastor—and thought I was an intellectual—I had a sermon where I couldn't bring myself to say the word *Devil* or *Satan*. Us intellectuals, we just didn't believe in stuff like that. Every place where the word Satan should have appeared in the sermon, I substituted the phrase *metaphorical personification of evil*. And the dear people in that congregation must have thought, *Say what? Metaphorical personification of evil?*

I'm a lot older and a little wiser now, and Satan has become a familiar acquaintance. He is personal, he is real, and he is out to eat your lunch. Let me tell you something else: Satan doesn't want you to be free. Well-known Bible teacher Ron Dunn says, "If you didn't meet the Devil this morning, it's a pretty good indication that the two of you are going in the same direction." Satan has somehow changed the definitions on us: He has made a lot of us believe that there is something spiritual about saying how horrible we are; something spiritual about failure; about self-abasement; about submission to the wrong people; about allowing yourself to be manipulated. He is wrong in every case. There is absolutely nothing spiritual about any of those things.

Christians are not dualists.

You say, "I'm glad to hear that! All my life I've wanted to know whether or not we were dualists!"

Dualists are those who believe that the world is controlled by two equal and opposing powers—one good and the other bad. It's what we see in Eastern religions, with their concepts of yin and yang. There is good and evil; there is love and hate; there is male and female. Many Christians have incorporated that kind of thinking into their own theology. We have said that Satan is bad, and God is good . . . and we must cast the deciding vote.

That is nonsense. Christianity is not dualistic. There is only one God, and Satan is nothing more than His lackey. Look at the first chapters of Job and you will see it. Every time you stand against Satan, all the powers of God's angelic hosts come to your aid. You have great power as a child of God. God does not allow Satan to do anything to you that doesn't first pass through a nail-scarred hand.

"I'm All Alone in My Pain"

There is one more lie to examine before we end this chapter. Lie number five: *I'm the only one who knows this prison and feels this pain.* The apostle Peter calls us on this one:

> Dear friends, do not be surprised at the painful trial you are suffering, as though something strange were happening to you. (1 Peter 4:12 NIV)

Scripture teaches over and over again that we all share a commonality of experience. Yet all too often we begin to think that we are the only one suffering a particular pain.

I got my clinical training at the Harvard Experimental Hospital, and took the required psychology courses at Boston University. When I got out of seminary, I hung up a little plaque that said, "Steve Brown, Boy Psychologist." Very quickly, I began to learn that I was not called to this kind of work. But because my ministry has been pretty unconventional—because people in my churches have always sensed that, "If Steve could do it, a monkey could do it," and that, "If Steve is that bad, I can tell him anything about me"—because I do have those kinds of "credentials," I have always had a very large counseling ministry.

I've probably made a lot of people feel better, even though I may not have helped them very much. But there's one thing I have always liked about counseling. As I have listened to other Christians talk, I have begun to realize that I was normal! I have begun to realize that everyone else is just like me. Frightened like me, and lonely like me. I've realized that there are people who love Christ who are struggling in the same way I'm struggling. By listening to other people I've found out that I am normal.

A number of years ago, when I was in my forties (I'm fifty-two as I write this), like most guys in their forties I went through a mid-life crisis. I got a call one morning from a man who said, "Steve, I've got to talk to you."

I said, "What's up?"

He said, "I'm having a nervous breakdown."

Because I knew this man, and knew that he wasn't the type who had nervous breakdowns, I said, "There's no such thing as a nervous breakdown; it's called by something else. That is layman's language. When you talk to somebody as sophisticated as I am, you need to describe your condition in more clear terminology. What do you mean, you're 'having a nervous breakdown?'"

He said, "Well, for a number of nights now, I have found myself waking up at two or three in the morning in a cold sweat of panic. And I begin to worry about my death. And I worry about everything in my life, about being sick. And I can't go back to sleep. I start shaking and it's awful."

I said to him, "I did that last night."

He said, "What?"

I said, "The problem is that we are in our forties. That's just some of the stuff you feel when you go through mid-life crisis."

He said, "No kidding! That makes me feel better! You do the same thing!"

We formed a "mid-life crisis fellowship of guys that wake up at three in the morning." It was so nice to know that others did it too.

Are you afraid sometimes? Do you sometimes feel really guilty? I feel guilty sometimes too.

Do you have trouble with the normal Christian life? Me too.

Have you ever sinned? Me too.

The seven-year statute of limitations hasn't run out and you are afraid that someone is going to catch you? I've been there.

You can't sleep sometimes? I can't sleep sometimes.

Do people intimidate you sometimes? Yes, people intimidate me sometimes too. *You* intimidate me sometimes! So that makes you normal, and that makes me normal.

I sometimes tell the seminary students, "If you are preaching and make a very good point to a congregation, you will probably get a 70 or 75 percent response. You will never get a hundred percent, because nobody makes a point that good. Some people are going to keep looking out the window."

I won't give that advice much anymore, however, because the other night I just about got a hundred percent response. A group of professional singles had been studying my book, *When Being Good Isn't Good Enough*.[3] They invited me to their last session to answer questions. I guess there were a hundred or a hundred fifty singles in that room. While answering questions about the book, I made an off-the-cuff remark: "Everyone here has something in his or her life which, if it were revealed to everyone else in this room, they would look for the nearest bridge." Looking around the room, I knew that I had gotten a hundred percent of them! Everyone in that room knew exactly what I was talking about.

You are normal. You are not the only one in the prison and you are not the only one facing the pain. As a matter of fact, the prison and the pain are universal.

As I awakened one morning the room started going around. My heart started beating rapidly. I thought I was having a heart attack. So at the insistence of Anna, I went to see Dr. McGowan, who is in heaven now. I said, "Doc, I'm having a heart attack and I think I'm going to die."

He said, "Describe your symptoms."

I did. And do you know what he did? He gave me a paper bag.

I said, "Doc, wait just a second! I mean, I'm paying you a lot of money! I'm having a heart attack and you give me a paper bag?"

He said, "You weren't having a heart attack, you were hyperventilating. Next time you feel that way, breathe into this bag. The problem was that you were getting too much oxygen."

I thank God to this day that the doctor did that for me. If he had told me it was serious, and that he was going to run a number of tests, I would still be hyperventilating. But I never hyperventilated again, because my doctor said I was normal.

So be assured: Whatever your problem, whatever your situation, you are normal.

If you have read any of my other books or attended my seminars, you may know that I am afraid of flying. I used to think that I was the only one with this fear. A friend of mine who was the head pilot of a major airline put me through a flight safety program. I flew a simulator DC-10 and went through a lot of instruction. After two nights of this my friend said, "Now, Steve, don't you feel better?"

I replied, "Are you crazy! I never knew so much could go wrong with an airplane!"

One time I was at a motel at the Philadelphia airport. I had my travel alarm clock set, but that morning, for some reason, I awakened early. I thought, *I can catch an earlier flight if I get on out to the airport.* So I picked up the travel alarm and put it in my attaché case, ran out the door, over to the airport, and got an earlier flight.

Now, what I didn't remember was that I had forgotten to un-set the alarm. When we got up to about thirty thousand feet, that alarm clock went off in my attaché case. You know all those people who look so cool when they fly? Well, they're not! There was a man reading the *Wall Street Journal* and he threw it up in the air. The girl in front of me screamed. It seemed like everyone in the plane was scared to death.

What am I saying? Welcome to the club!

Don't believe the lies. Don't believe the first lie: *I'm not in prison, and there is no pain.* Remember that you are in prison, and there is pain. Remember that you are a sinner and a bad one, just like me.

Don't believe the second lie: *I must accept the prison and the pain.* No, you don't have to accept the prison or the pain.

Don't believe lie number three: *I deserve the prison and the pain.* Well, yes you do, but Jesus doesn't and you are in Christ—so you deserve royal treatment.

Don't believe lie number four: *I can't change the prison and the pain.* We saw that, quite to the contrary, we are living in a supernatural world—and God has given you and me great power to deal with whatever the supernatural world throws our way.

And whatever you do, don't ever believe that final lie: *I'm the only one who knows the prison and feels the pain.* We're all in this together. We're all human and we're all sinners. And grace always runs downhill.

If you keep that in mind, you're going to make some real progress.

5

Finding Your Way Out of Prison

To be honest with you, as I started working on this book I was working on some issues in my own life. I was feeling like some sort of special case—until I started talking with other people and found out that they were dealing with similar issues. If they were to have a national convention of children of normal parents, nobody would come! Because of the Fall, we all deal with our issues. In this chapter, after taking another look at how we got into our prisons, we're going to start looking at some ways to get out. We'll talk about that more in chapters 6 through 8—especially in chapter 8—but we can begin talking about it now. Once you are in a prison and you have identified your prison, how do you find your way out?

That was precisely the problem the Israelites faced in this passage from 1 Samuel:

> And all the people said to Samuel, "Pray for your servants to the LORD your God, that we may not die; for we have added to all our sins the evil of asking a king for ourselves." Then Samuel said to the people, "Do not fear. You have done all this wickedness; yet do not turn aside from following the LORD, but serve the LORD with all your heart. And do not turn aside; for then you would go after empty things which cannot profit or deliver, for they are nothing. For the LORD will not forsake His people, for His great name's sake, because it has pleased the LORD to make you His people. Moreover, as for

me, far be it from me that I should sin against the LORD in
ceasing to pray for you; but I will teach you the good and the
right way. Only fear the LORD, and serve Him in truth with all
your heart; for consider what great things He has done for
you. But if you still do wickedly, you shall be swept away,
both you and your king." (1 Samuel 12:19–25)

An earlier passage in 1 Samuel (8:6–9) shows that God
considered the Israelites' desire for a king as a rejection of
His divine kingship. Now, having chosen themselves a king,
the Israelites apparently realize they have made the wrong
choice. Having gotten themselves on the wrong road, they
want to get back on the right road. Having gotten themselves
into a prison of their own making, they wanted out.

It's a good thing no one tried to tell the Israelites about
codependency! That's a word you've probably heard a lot
lately. I certainly came across it often as I read some seventy
or eighty books in preparation for the seminar this book was
based on. I have concluded that *codependency* is just another
way of talking about the Fall. The problem with the recovery
movement is that the recovery movement itself can become
an addiction. It can become just another manifestation of the
Fall.

One day a lawyer, who later became my friend, called me
and said, "I want you to come over and talk with me . . .
because somebody told me you were a straight shooter . . .
and I have a booze problem and I need somebody to talk to
me straight."

I said, "I'm not going over there. You come over here."

He said, "I want you to come here."

I said, "I'm busy. I'm not going there. If you want some
help, you come here."

Now, that is a psychological technique: making people
pay or take some other kind of initiative, so that it becomes
important to them.

So then he said, "Reverend, can I tell you the truth?"

I said, "Sure."

He said, "I'm drunk, and I'm ashamed to go out of the house. I'd get killed driving over there. And I don't want anyone at the church to see what I look like, so would you please come over here?"

I went to his house and he was drunk. Drunk as a skunk. Not only that, but he had a .38 sitting on the coffee table, right beside his glass of booze. He said, "I want you to tell me what will help."

I said, "Let me tell you something: You are so drunk that if I told you now, you wouldn't remember it in the morning. So I'm not going to tell you anything right now."

He said, "Yes, you are."

I said, "No, I'm not. If you can stay sober for three days, then I'll tell you something that will help. But until you get sober, you're not going to remember anything I say to you."

He said, "I want you to tell me right now."

I looked at that .38 and decided, "Lord, if he asks me one more time, I'm going to tell him."

But he didn't.

Do you know what he did? It about killed him, but for the first time in about twenty years he got sober. He was sober for three days, so I went back over to his house. He couldn't even hold a glass, his hand was shaking so much. I presented Christ to him. I told him about how Jesus loved him. Then in a very beautiful and wonderful way he received Christ into his life.

You know what happened then? He promptly got drunk again and stayed drunk for a long time. He did finally get sober, and he hasn't had a drink for years. But recently he became addicted to Valium. He was so proud that he hadn't had a drink for so long, but he had just made a substitution.

That is what much of the recovery movement is. A lot of it is very helpful in terms of the analysis of the problem, but the recovery movement itself can become another addiction.

The recovery movement asks the right questions, but it doesn't give real and lasting answers. When you are driving your car and making real good time . . . but going the wrong way . . . it is not an accomplishment, it is a tragedy. There are a lot of truths in the recovery movement—true because, as I will show you, they are biblical. But the truths are merely stepping stones toward freedom, not rocks to build your house on.

Pretty soon we're going to look at some solid steps that will unlock our prison doors—not just lock us into an endless cycle of recovery. But first we need to gain a little more understanding as to how we got into our prisons in the first place.

Becoming Prisoners: The Man on the Tack

The subhead for this section may make you think it's a repetition of chapter 2, but it isn't. You should find some new insights here. The things we're going to look at now are not excuses for being in prison, but aids in understanding the road that got us there and the things that keep us there. Take them seriously, but don't make them the focus of your life.

Have you heard about the man sitting on the tack? A psychologist came along, saw that the man was obviously in pain, and said, "The reason you hurt so much is that you were potty-trained wrong. You're from a dysfunctional family; you've always had this fear of abandonment. That's why it hurts so much."

Then a teacher came along and said, "The reason you hurt is that you are uneducated."

A sociologist came along and said, "The reason you hurt so much is because of your social situation. You have a bad self-image and it has caused you to get involved with improper social institutions—and that's why you hurt so much."

A preacher came along and said, "Do you know why you hurt so much? It's because you don't pray enough and you don't read your Bible enough and you don't go to church enough."

Then a little boy came along and said, "It hurts, doesn't it? Do you know why it hurts so much?"

The man said, "No, I don't."

The little boy said, "Because you're sitting on a tack! Get off the tack!"

So let's take a look at the wrong road many of us have taken. Let's examine the "tack" we're sitting on. But as we do this, we are not going to become enamored with the tack. The purpose of showing you the tack is to show you how to get *off* the tack.

Most of the dysfunctional "tacks" we suffer from are multi-generational. Most of our prisons are from the past:

> For I, the LORD your God, am a jealous God, visiting the iniquity of the fathers upon the children to the third and fourth generations of those who hate Me, but showing mercy to thousands, to those who love Me and keep My commandments. (Exodus 20:5–6)

That doesn't mean God is so ticked at you that He is out to get your children and your grandchildren and your great-grandchildren. It simply means that this is the way the world works. Wrong roads were taken several generations back, and you were born on the wrong road. I was born on the wrong road, too. My grandfather's suicide is a part of the multi-generational dysfunction in my life.

Your "Child" Is Lost

To understand how you got into prison, the *first* thing you need to realize, therefore, is that *your child is lost and needs to be found*. I'm using the term "child" in the way it is often used in popular psychology, to refer, not to your son or daughter, but to those things from your own childhood that still affect your life as an adult. We can be pretty sure that King David never read a recovery book or attended a twelve-step or codependency seminar, but he did understand something about multi-generational family dysfunctions. As he looks at the sin in his own life, David states a "fact of life" that we often ignore at our own peril:

> Behold, I was brought forth in iniquity,
> And in sin my mother conceived me. (Psalm 51:5)

Why don't we simply get off the tack? Because each of us, individually, was born as a sinner into a fallen world. Someone has told us that sitting on the tack is proper and right. Consciously or unconsciously, you were initiated into a "tack fellowship."

My mother used to tell me that I was going to be just like my father, who was a drunk. As a family we spent most of our time trying to cover for my father with lies and crazy stories. Shame became a way of life for me. The possibility of discovery became a horrible fear. My mother sometimes felt like she had "had it up to her ears" with my drunken father, and she would threaten to leave. So I also had a fear of abandonment. In order to deal with my prisons, I had to go back and understand some of the things in the past. I had to find my lost child.

Most dysfunctions are multi-generational; most prisons come from your past.

Family Sins Are Repeated

The second key to understanding your imprisonment is to realize that *the sin and the pain are repeated from generation to generation*. Unfortunately, this biographical note about one of Israel's minor kings is not at all unusual or surprising:

> In the eighteenth year of King Jeroboam the son of Nebat, Abijam became king over Judah. He reigned three years in Jerusalem. His mother's name was Maachah the grand-daughter of Abishalom. And he walked in all the sins of his

father, which he had done before him; his heart was not loyal to the LORD his God. (1 Kings 15:1–3)

The book of 2 Kings tells of nineteen consecutive evil kings who ruled Israel, leading up to the nation's defeat and captivity by Assyria. About each of them it could be said, "Like father, like son." As the prophet Jeremiah said,

> The fathers have eaten sour grapes,
> And the children's teeth are set on edge. (Jeremiah 31:29)

Or as Jesus said in Matthew 23:31–32:

> Therefore you are witnesses against yourselves that you are sons of those who murdered the prophets. Fill up, then, the measure of your fathers' guilt.

Or as He said in John 8:41:

> You do the deeds of your father.

We tend to repeat our family's sinful, dysfunctional, and destructive experiences. I keep saying, "I'm never going to be like my father." Yet as I get older, I see more and more how like my father I am.

Why do we tend to repeat our family's sin? Psychologists give lots of reasons. Some say we do it because we need to go back to correct what has been wrong—trying to get it right this time. Maybe it is a learned behavior. Maybe we do it in an effort to understand.

None of those explanations or proposed solutions sound very logical. But why should they? Getting on the tack in the first place is not logical! The Bible recognizes the absurdity and hopelessness of our imprisonment to generational sins, and shows clearly that the only possible solution is a supernatural one:

For thus says the LORD:

"Your affliction is incurable,
Your wound is severe.
There is no one to plead your cause,
That you may be bound up;
You have no healing medicines.
All your lovers have forgotten you;
They do not seek you;
For I have wounded you with the wound of an enemy,
With the chastisement of a cruel one,
For the multitude of your iniquities,
Because your sins have increased.
Why do you cry about your affliction?
Your sorrow is incurable.
Because of the multitude of your iniquities,
Because your sins have increased,
I have done these things to you." (Jeremiah 30:12–15)

Now, that is total helplessness! But I can hardly wait to show you the next two verses:

"Therefore all those who devour you shall be devoured;
And all your adversaries, every one of them, shall go into
   captivity;
Those who plunder you shall become plunder,
And all who prey upon you I will make a prey.
For I will restore health to you
And heal you of your wounds," says the LORD. (verses 16–17)

We are learning about the past so that we will understand it, *not* so that we can fix it. Only God can fix it. I have found that Christian counseling is often simply a place to identify one's helplessness. One time after I had prayed with a man, he asked, with a big smile, "What happened?"

I said, "I don't know."

He said, "Something happened. What happened?"

I replied, "God happened."

As my friend Larry Crabb says, you must keep probing at the problem until you get to the pain that only God can fix.

False Guilt and Futile Remedies

There's a third process that helps put a lot of us into prison. We have noted that family sins are often repeated from one generation to the next. Sometimes, however, it is just the feelings of guilt—not the actual sin—that is inherited. Because of our past dysfunctional situations or traumatic experiences, we feel unworthy and guilty even though we have done nothing wrong—or at least nothing to warrant that much guilt. When that happens, *futile remedies are tried for the false guilt*.

An ordinary dictionary would define *guilt* as the realization that you have done wrong according to some ethical, moral, or religious standard. Often, along with such a realization comes lowered self-esteem and a feeling that you should make restitution for the wrong you have done.

In psychoanalytic writings, on the other hand, the term *guilt* usually refers to neurotic, unreasonable, or pathological guilt feelings that do not appear to be justified by the reasons given for those feelings. You feel guilty even though you have done nothing wrong.

Healthy guilt is what you feel after you have violated a legitimate, clearly revealed and understood biblical standard, that is, when you did something bad and you feel bad and you *ought to* feel bad—because you did something bad. Unhealthy guilt, on the other hand, involves feeling bad even though you are not aware of having violated a standard.

Dealing with actual guilt is a healthy thing to do, and it follows a logical and healthy pattern:

1. First, you violate the teaching or principle and recognize that you have done so.

2. Second, this realization makes you feel guilty.

3. Third, you get the punishment. (If you are a child, your mother spanks you.)

4. And then—the fourth and final step—there is release and freedom.

With unhealthy or false guilt, items one and four are removed. In other words:

2. You feel guilty (step two) even though you haven't done anything wrong (step one).

3. Then, you try to punish yourself (step three) so that you can get free (step four).

2 & 3. But the self-punishment only makes you feel even more guilty, so you go back and forth between steps two and three—between the false guilt feelings and the self-punishment—and you never reach step four.

When I was a young pastor, a prostitute came to me for counseling. I began to probe, trying to find out about her past. I had just gotten my training at Harvard, and felt fairly self-confident. As we began to talk, I learned that when she was a very little girl, before the age of verbalization, her mother had undergone a lobotomy and was institutionalized as a vegetable for the rest of her life. And her father, who couldn't take care of his little girl because he had to make a living, placed her with two unmarried aunts.

As she began living with the aunts, she began to feel unworthy. She felt that it was an awful situation and that she was a terrible person. She felt guilty (step two) even though she had done nothing wrong (step one). Her eventual career of prostitution was her self-imposed punishment (step three) for this false guilt (step two). "If I get hurt enough," she reasoned, "then I won't feel guilty and I'll be free."

But all she did was feel more and more guilty. Of course her prostitution also brought *true* guilt into her life. But she never was able to get free of the false guilt that had started it all. All she did was keep going back and forth between step two and step three—from false guilt, to punishment, to more false guilt, and so forth.

I could give you dozens of examples of that process. There was another young lady who was in some horrible prisons of guilt. As we began to probe, she told me that her mother had been raped while she, the daughter, was in her own room down the hall—and she had slept through the whole thing. The young lady told me in counseling that she had even opened the door for the rapist. I checked the police records; I checked with her mother; and the story simply was not true. Yet somehow this young woman had gotten the feeling that she was responsible for all the trauma in her home. And so she started going back and forth between guilt and punishment, guilt and punishment.

Now, don't forget: The healthy way to deal with guilt is:

1. You violate something important and you recognize that you have done so.

2. You feel guilty about it.

3. You get punished.

4. You find release and freedom.

But if it is unhealthy and unreasonable guilt, then you go back and forth between two and three. You feel guilty and you get punished. You feel more guilty and you get punished again. False guilt, inherited from your family or from whatever other source, can lead you to pursue needless and futile remedies.

Your Problems Tend to Increase

Then fourthly, you can be kept in prison because *the problems and needs that put you there in the first place tend to grow bigger the longer they go unaddressed.* Jesus told a parable about the danger of failing to address areas of need in our lives:

> When an unclean spirit goes out of a man, he goes through dry places, seeking rest, and finds none. Then he says, "I will return to my house from which I came." And when he comes, he finds it empty, swept, and put in order. Then he goes and takes with him seven other spirits more wicked than himself, and they enter and dwell there; and the last state of that man is worse than the first. So shall it also be with this wicked generation. (Matthew 12:43–45)

The demon is cast out; the void is left unfilled; the problem becomes seven times worse.

Jeremiah may well have been thinking of neglected problems growing worse by the day as he penned this sad lament:

> The harvest is past,
> The summer is ended,
> And we are not saved. (Jeremiah 8:20)

Needs are often magnified in our lives simply by benign neglect, that is, by pretending the need is not there. This is especially a problem with men. Many of my male counselees simply don't want to deal with problems. If they are well-fed and comfortable, they don't want to make waves. Unless forced to, men never deal with feelings.

For that very reason, men tend to stay in their prisons longer than women do. You don't just "grow out of" prisons; they become worse. It is the "second law of spiritual dynamics." A Pharisee will remain so and become better at it. A harmful habit will not just go away, it will become more harmful. Unresolved failure will not turn into success, it will turn into more failure.

I said to myself, just before resigning from the church, "At least it can't get worse." But it did.

I had been a pastor for twenty-eight years and, to be

honest with you, I had done a not-half-bad job of it. The problem was not in my teaching (I checked, and was sure I had been teaching truth), or in my commitment (you've never met anyone who wanted to be a good pastor more than I did). The problem was that I had never dealt with those sleeping dogs in my life.

Rather, I have covered them with good, hard, religious work for God. I was getting up at four in the morning and often working until midnight or long after. I was trying to be a full-time pastor to a congregation while, at the same time, traveling more than 125 days a year to speak at conferences, colleges, and churches. I was doing five "Key Life" broadcasts a week, hours of counseling, and preaching at the church where I served three times a week. I was also trying to be the kind of husband and father God had called me to be.

Finally, the "butter began to slip off my cracker." I came to the realization that something had to give. So, after a great amount of turmoil, I resigned my pastorate, started teaching at the seminary, and continued my work with Key Life.

I thought I had died and gone to heaven!

That's when God began to teach me how I had covered my fear and shame with religiosity. That was also when He showed me that I would either deal with those sleeping dogs—those unresolved issues of my past—or get worse.

Those days were quite painful. And the pain got worse before it got better. Out of those days—perhaps out of my "misery-loves-company" instinct—came the "Born Free" seminars that form the basis of this book.

Bitterness Tends to Increase

The fifth thing you need to understand is that *prisons create bitterness, and bitterness creates more bitterness*. Bitterness tends very quickly to get out of control. That's why the warning in Hebrews 12:15 is still so relevant twenty centuries after it was given:

> . . . looking carefully lest anyone fall short of the grace of God;
> lest any root of bitterness springing up cause trouble, and by
> this many become defiled.

People fall short of God's grace because of bitterness. You can't resolve the bitterness inside until you recognize and name that bitterness and bring it into the light.

Have you ever been angry and bitter at God? Well, you probably should have been, at some time or other in your life! Bitterness is sometimes the first step toward healing. But don't forget how easily it can get out of hand, as it seems to have for Job:

> I cry out to You, but You do not answer me;
> I stand up, and You regard me.
> But You have become cruel to me;
> With the strength of Your hand You oppose me.
> You lift me up to the wind and cause me to ride on it;
> You spoil my success.
> For I know that You will bring me to death. (Job 30:20–23)

"Frankly, I'm tired of it," says Job. "And I know, Lord, that Your ultimate goal is to destroy me." As with Job, so with us: It's hard to put a lid on bitterness. You can't just let it stay there.

My mother was once in a coma for three days. While in the coma, she would often thrash about and it would take three of us to hold her down. I remember one nurse telling me, at three o'clock one morning, "Mr. Brown, I don't know if she's getting stronger or I'm getting weaker, but I don't think I can keep this up."

The interesting thing about my mother's coma is that almost all the time she was unconscious, she prayed. One nurse remarked that she "had heard them cuss, cry out, and be angry, but I've never heard that kind of prayer."

My mother prayed lots of things during that coma, but the one phrase she repeated over and over again was, "Lord, help me to forgive. Help me not to hold anything against anyone anymore."

I have often wondered about my mother's spiritual power and freedom. I used to think it was because she was consistent in her Bible reading, or because she was active in church, or because she helped people, or because she read Spurgeon. Those things surely helped. But the real secret of her spiritual power and freedom was her refusal to bear bitterness toward anyone.

We Tend to Deceive and Deny

Sixthly, you need to understand *how deceitful you and I are and how easily we deny the truth.* Jeremiah 17:9 says:

The heart is deceitful above all things. . . . Who can know it?

One of the most dangerous kinds of denial is denying the pain in your life. Did you hear about the three people who went to hell? One was a Baptist, one was a Presbyterian, and one was a Christian Scientist. The Baptist said, "If I had listened to my pastor when he gave the plan of salvation, I wouldn't be here."

The Presbyterian said, "If I had listened to my pastor teach about grace, I wouldn't be here."

The Christian Scientist, meanwhile, was over in the corner with his head in his hands, saying, "It's not hot and I'm not here. It's not hot and I'm not here."

One of the great things about the Cross is that we don't have to be right anymore. We don't have to be good anymore. We don't have to cover up anymore. We are forgiven.

We've all got our problems. We're all from bad backgrounds. Now that we've got that straight, can we talk?

You're a sinner. I'm a sinner. There is no sin of which you and I are not capable. Now that that is straight, can we talk?

You and I fail a lot. We're not super-Christians. We are

frightened and wounded and sometimes we are very lonely. Now that that is straight, can we talk?

I had a friend who started out as my enemy. I felt, every time I was around him, that he was judging me. Sometimes it was just a feeling, and other times he was quite verbal with his criticism. One day, by accident, I found out something of his background. I realized the secrets he was trying to hide. So I went to him.

"Bill," I said, "let me tell you something about me that I think you ought to know." I told him one of my "dark secrets"—one that was sort of like his. "The problem," I said, "is that every time I'm around you, I have this feeling that you know me, that you don't like me, and that you will tell everyone you know all about me."

Do you know what happened? He started crying. He told me that the reason he was so critical of me was that, as long as he could direct his and others' attention to me, nobody would look at him. "Steve," he said, "I'm so ashamed."

That was when we got honest and, right now, I have no better friend in the world, nor any I trust more.

You can't deny the pain.

We Play Unrealistic Roles

Finally, point number seven, we get into our prisons and stay there by *playing roles that are not reality.* Jesus recognized that the self-righteous Pharisees were merely playing a role:

> Woe to you, scribes and Pharisees, hypocrites! For you cleanse the outside of the cup and dish, but inside they are full of extortion and self-indulgence. Blind Pharisee, first cleanse the inside of the cup and dish, that the outside of them may be clean also. Woe to you, scribes and Pharisees, hypocrites! For you are like whitewashed tombs which indeed appear beautiful outwardly, but inside are full of dead men's bones and all uncleanness. Even so you also outwardly appear righteous to men, but inside you are full of hypocrisy and lawlessness. (Matthew 23:25–28)

The Pharisees played a role that did not match the reality of what was in their hearts. Let's look at some of the roles that you and I sometimes play. I'll name the roles and then use incidents from the life of the apostle Peter to illustrate each role. (If he could have played all these roles, how many of them might you or I be playing!)

First, there is Heroic Howard and Rescuer Rita. Peter played that role at least once:

> Peter said to Him, "Lord, why can I not follow You now? I will lay down my life for Your sake."

To which Jesus replied,

> Will you lay down your life for My sake? Most assuredly, I say to you, the rooster shall not crow till you have denied Me three times. (John 13:37–38)

I mean, Peter wanted to get in there and fix it. He wanted to be a rescuer of Jesus. Do you play that role? Do you want to fix every problem? Rescue every hurt soul in the world? You can't do it.

The second role is Martyred Marvin and Poor Patty. Peter said, "Lord, how often shall my brother sin against me, and I forgive him? Up to seven times?" (Matthew 18:21).

Do you ever play that role? Have you ever been the martyr? "I'll take whatever they give me and deal with it, because I'm a Christian."

Then there's Humble Harry (whom we met in chapter 1) and Worthless Wanda. "Peter said to Him, 'You shall never wash my feet!'" (John 13:8).

Do you ever say, "I'm just a worm?" Perhaps you're always focusing on all your past mistakes, and all the while reaffirming your conviction that, "I'm an awful, terrible, worthless amoeba."

Then there is the role of Pretty Paula and Perfect Paul. The text says,

Now when Peter had come to Antioch, I withstood him to his face, because he was to be blamed; for before certain men came from James, he would eat with the Gentiles; but when they came, he withdrew and separated himself, fearing those who were of the circumcision. (Galatians 2:11–12)

In other words, Peter wanted to please everyone. He wanted to be perfect. He wanted to live up to everyone's standards.

And there's the role of Silent Sally and Bland Billy. Peter plays this role in John 21:3: "Simon Peter said to them, 'I am going fishing.'" In other words, I'm just going to bear my horrible pain alone.

Have you ever done that?

Those are all false roles. Roles that prisoners play. One of the keys to freedom is to reject the false roles that you have accepted.

Let's review quickly: We get into our prisons and stay there because:

• Each of us, individually, was born as a sinner into a fallen world. We were all born "sitting on a tack."

• Sin and pain tend to be repeated from generation to generation.

• We try futile remedies for the false guilt we have inherited.

• The problems and needs that put us in prison in the first place tend to grow bigger when unaddressed.

• Prisons create bitterness, and bitterness, when not dealt with, rapidly increases.

• We humans tend to be deceitful; we tend to deny the truth.

- Finally, we get into prison and stay there by playing unrealistic roles.

So that's how we got into our prisons. How do we get out?

R E F L E C T: Getting Out of Prison

For the Christian, there is a road back, and you can find it with the acrostic *R E F L E C T.* As we look at what those seven letters represent, we'll want to keep in mind three principles:

One: If sin is endemic to the human race (and it is), reason dictates that forgiveness and restoration must involve not only ourselves, but also our parents and sometimes even our grandparents.

Two: God molds us and modifies us with circumstances, especially family circumstances.

Three: God is interested not only in what is happening to you right now, but in what has happened to you in your past.

Now, one more thing before we proceed: A lot of you are rejecting what I'm saying right now, thinking it certainly doesn't apply to you. Let me suggest that, if you have recently caught yourself saying any of the following things, all this talk about prisons may indeed apply to you:

Have you recently caught yourself saying things like,

- "I don't remember much of my childhood."

- "I don't understand why I do what I do."

- "I do so many stupid things and my besetting sin is always there."

- "I'm worthless."

- "I can't achieve a loving, intimate relationship with those closest to me."

- "I'm constantly worried and anxiety-ridden, even when there's nothing to worry about."

- "I seem to feel responsible for all the Third World disasters."

- "I often live in extremes."

- "I am extremely obedient to authority figures," or,

- "I am extremely rebellious."

- "I always feel like something is missing in my life."

Those kinds of statements almost always reveal a familial prison. So let's look at that acrostic, *R E F L E C T*, and see what it can tell us about getting out of prison. The letters stand for: recognize, elucidate, forgive, liberate, eulogize, cage (or, take captive), and finally, give thanks.

First, *recognize*: We are going to learn a lot more about this later on, but denial is a major problem with those who want to be free and are not. That denial affects not just how we think about ourselves, but how we think about our parents. John Bradshaw, who writes and conducts workshops as a part of the recovery movement, is wrong about so many things, but he is right about one thing and that is the necessity of recognizing the "lost child" inside us. I didn't discover that intellectually but emotionally.

Let me tell you what happened to me. Bradshaw, in his workshops, leads a number of "meditations," and in one, he invites people to go back and speak to the child of their past. I was listening to some Bradshaw tapes in order to prepare for this book. When he started the soft music and went into the meditation I said to myself, *I don't need this stuff. I want the cognitive stuff.* I reached over to turn off the tape but I decided, *What the heck, I'll let it run.*

The music began to play. Bradshaw said, "I want you to go back to a place where as a child you were comfortable. Maybe in a swing or in your backyard." He said, "I want you to imagine approaching your child, and I want you to say to your child, 'Hello, I am what you are to become. I am the only one in the world who understands what you are going through right now. And I would like to visit you sometime if that would be all right with you.'"

As I listened to this meditation, I began crying. I didn't understand why I was crying until I began to realize that I had struck a mother lode. Something was going on in my childhood that I didn't understand. Let me suggest that you, along with Christ, visit your past. Ask God to help you remember the input of your past. Then, ask Him to reveal the reality of what has been done to you. Remember that (back to the multi-generational dysfunction and pain) what was done to you was probably also done to your parents and to their parents as well.

Second, *elucidate***:** It is desperately important that you meditate on and think about the truths about your past: the high demands of your parents; hypercriticism; verbal abuse; threats of abandonment; words of destruction; how love was given and withdrawn; how you were motivated; and so on.

Events are just events. Learning the significance of events is another thing altogether. For instance, I have always known that my father was an alcoholic. It was the focal point of our family. However, I always figured that the past was past and that it was better to turn away from the past by living fully in the present and looking forward to the future.

That sounds good, but it simply isn't possible. It was only as I looked at my father's alcoholism in terms of its effect on our family in general and on me in particular that I began to understand why I am the way I am. For instance, I have a great fear of shame. I have nightmares about making a fool of myself in public and being ashamed. So, I work very hard at controlling people and situations. Sometimes that control can be very painful to others.

It was only as I saw where my need to control came from that I was able to get some "control over my control." I am learning to let go and to no longer feel that everything must be "fixed" about me or about other people.

When you *elucidate* the past, you meditate on how the past has affected your present.

Third, *forgive***:** Contrary to most current psychological theories, forgiveness is necessary for any Christian who wants to deal with his or her past. You need to forgive *yourself* for having bought into your parents' neurotic trips. You need to also forgive *them* for having passed those neuroses on to you.

Confrontation and anger are unavoidable parts of the forgiveness process. This kind of forgiveness is not easy, and we are going to talk about that. Perhaps you need to write a letter that you never send. Perhaps you need to actually go to your parents. Picture yourself: A friend of mine went and stood beside the grave and talked to his father about all the things that had been done to him. If you were to do such a thing, you would begin to understand that your parents had some things done to them as well—that the problems are multi-generational. Be that as it may, however, *you* have to forgive.

Fourth, *liberate***:** Give yourself the permission to be free. Say, "If the Son has made me free, I'm free indeed" (see John 8:36). "I'm not bound by what has been said to me in the past and, in the name of Christ, I reject all of the past untruths of my life." Jesus said to His own parents—not unkindly—"I must be about My Father's business." His Father's business was love and grace.

At one of our seminars, a woman came to me after the three grueling days of growing and learning (our seminars are fun, but they are also hard work!). She was laughing and crying at the same time.

"I didn't know," she said, "I just didn't know. From now on, on the authority of God's revealed truth, I'm going to be free. I've been living as if God were my policeman. I thought that because my parents told me that He was. Every time I did something wrong, they made it clear that they were not pleased and never would be and, because they weren't pleased, God wasn't either.

"Now I know the truth about how much God loves me. Not only that, He *likes* me! And if that is true, I'm not going to play games anymore. I'm going to say things I shouldn't say and I'm never, ever, going to fit into anyone else's mold again."

She had given herself the permission to be free.

Fifth, *eulogize*: We Christians don't believe much in the mourning process but, believe me, it is important. You're going to be giving up some myths by which you have lived most of your life. You are going to be burying the perfect parents who never existed. You are going to say goodbye to a home, even an unhealthy one, in which you have lived for a long time. If that process makes you happy, you are a fruitcake! Mourning involves tears. It involves recognizing that you aren't fine. And that it hurts. And that sometimes it hurts really bad.

So don't be afraid to eulogize—cry, weep, go through the mourning process.

Sixth, *cage*, or *take captive*: Second Corinthians 10:3–4 is an interesting text:

> For though we walk in the flesh, we do not war according to the flesh. For the weapons of our warfare are not carnal but mighty in God for pulling down strongholds, casting down arguments and every high thing that exalts itself against the knowledge of God, . . .

And here it comes . . .

> . . . bringing every thought into captivity to the obedience of Christ.

Your mind controls your actions, and you control your mind. Even though we have been trying to get *out* of our prisons, imagine putting your past in a prison cell, locking it up, and walking away from it.

Most of us have "tapes" in our minds. Those tapes have been recorded with all kinds of spurious and negative ideas and thoughts about ourselves—thoughts such as: *I'm no good; I can never be anything; I ought to be ashamed; I'll die if people find out the way I really am.*

What I'm suggesting is not "positive thinking," but rather a re-recording of those tapes with the truth of Scripture. For instance, when you are wallowing in self-condemnation, learn to say, "'There is therefore now no condemnation to those who are in Christ Jesus' (Romans 8:1). If that is true, then I am acceptable to God and, if I'm acceptable to God, anyone who disagrees with God is a twit! I'm valuable. I'm loved. I'm empowered by the Holy Spirit."

Finally, *give thanks*: At the end of the process, you need to give God the thanks for this revelation of truth, and for the fact that His Son died to set you free. Without thanksgiving, there is no healing.

If God is sovereign (and He is), and if Romans 8:28 is true (and it is), then every circumstance of your life has been a part of God's bringing you to this point.

My friend and colleague Dave O'Dowd, pastor of Seminole Presbyterian Church in Tampa and adjunct professor at Reformed Seminary, was once approached by an angry young woman Dave had led to Christ some two months before.

"I'm mad," she said. "You never told me about all this stuff. You never told me about the tears and the pain I would encounter when Christ started working on me."

Dave replied, "Sara, would you rather not have known Him?"

She paused for a moment and thought. "No, knowing Christ is the most important thing in my life."

"Then," Dave said, "Tell Him, and thank Him for it."

Often, God waits for us to thank Him for the insight and freedom He offers. If we never thank Him, we have never understood. Thanksgiving is the final step and maybe the most important one.

Now, before we finish this chapter, I want to say a word about sexual abuse. No book has affected me more deeply than one by my friend Dan Allender, called *The Wounded Heart*.[4] If you have gone through sexual abuse, you should read that book. Then you should discuss it with a trusted Christian counselor. Sometimes those things are so heavy and so deep that they are not easy to deal with. None of this is easy to deal with, but when you have gone through sexual abuse, that is heavy stuff. So very rarely can someone who has been abused in that way handle all of these other things we've been talking about.

I want you to get the book, *The Wounded Heart*, and I want you to read it, and I want you to think about it. But even in sexual abuse, the *R E F L E C T* acrostic is still important: *R*—recognize, *E*—elucidate, *F*—forgive, *L*—liberate, *E*—eulogize, *C*—take captive, and the *T*—give thanks.

A friend of mine lived in the prison of her guilt for most

of her adult life. We talked for hours about some of the stuff out of which she had built her prison. She carried an old picture in her wallet of herself as a little girl and, sometimes when she was drunk or high, she would take that picture of her as a little girl, look at the picture, and start crying. Then she would say to the picture, "What have I done to that little girl?"

She is healthy now. She says, "I don't look at that picture much anymore. I have another question now that I am getting well. I say, 'What has that little girl done to me?'"

6

God's Nature Makes You Free

Now it's time for a mini-lesson in theology. I'm going to help you find your way out of prison by better understanding who God is and how He works. One of the major reasons Christians stay in prison is that they don't know theology.

You say, "Wait a minute, I don't want to know theology. I just want out of my prison."

Maybe you've heard the old saying that, "kissin' don't last, but cookin' do." Well, feelings don't last either, but doctrine does. That's why it is so important for us to find out what the Bible really says about God—not what someone else says, but what God says about Himself.

In his defenses of orthodox Christian theology, Francis Schaeffer often used the analogy of a two-story house. He said that the first story represents the realm of what he called "space-time" events—that is, things you and I can see happening in the world around us. The second story represents the implications we draw from those space-time events. For instance, on the first story you would find things like the actual, historical resurrection of Christ, when a dead man got up and walked. On the second story you find things like the fact that, because of Christ's resurrection, we are immortal. Schaeffer said the problem with theological liberals is that they want a second story without having a first story.

The Bible is revealed, propositional truth, not only about

spiritual implications but also about the actual historic events from which we draw those implications. Paul's letters always lay a doctrinal base before giving the practical implications. In Ephesians 1–3, for instance, you find a doctrinal base; in chapters 4–6 you find the practical implications of that doctrinal base.

In practical terms, you are probably still reading this book because you have identified some prisons you would like to get out of. But to reach that "second story" of liberation, you need to enter through the ground floor of theology, that is, the rock-solid facts of who God is and what He has done in the real world of human history.

The Nature of God

Let's talk about the nature of God. Stuart Briscoe recalls a time some years ago when he was flying all over the world telling people about Jesus. His wife, Jill, said to him, "There's a coffee house across the street; you ought to go over there and tell them about Christ."

Stuart put it off until finally one evening he didn't have anything else to do and he felt guilty, so he went over to the coffee house, which was called "The Cat's Whiskers." He sat down and started talking to a young man. When he finished presenting the gospel, the young man said, "You don't really believe this."

Stuart said, "What do you mean, I 'don't believe this?'"

He said, "If you really believed something that good, you would have been over here telling us about it long before now."

It is important to know about God, to know what we really believe and to know how really good it is. Here are some things we should know about God—some things about God that can help make us free.

God Is In Charge, You Aren't

If you want to be free you need, first of all, to know about the *rule* of God. *God is in charge, which means that you aren't in charge.* Paul makes this very clear in Romans 9:19–21:

You will say to me then, "Why does He still find fault? For who has resisted His will?" But indeed, O man, who are you to reply against God? Will the thing formed say to him who formed it, "Why have you made me like this?" Does not the potter have power over the clay?

And again in Romans 11:34–36:

For who has known the mind of the Lord?
Or who has become His counselor?
Or who has first given to Him
And it shall be repaid to him?

For of Him and through Him and to Him are all things, to whom be glory forever. Amen.

George Schweitzer, a friend of my friend Fred Smith, has a number of Ph.D.s, and was at one time an atheist. He says that by the time he finished his last Ph.D. he had made a list of what he considered to be the important questions of life. The first question on his list was, Is there a God? As Schweitzer explains, "If there is a God, He is in charge. If there isn't a God, then I'm in charge."

That is the issue for each of us: Who is in control—you, or God? R. C. Sproul, my colleague at the seminary, says, "If one molecule is not under the purview of the sovereignty of God, then everything is outside the purview of the sovereignty of God."

People sometimes tell me they have "intellectual questions" concerning the Christian faith. Yet with one or two significant exceptions, no one I have encountered in over thirty years of ministry has shown solid evidence of actually having serious intellectual questions. What they have had were some well-constructed smoke-screens. They keep asking the questions so that they don't have to surrender control of their lives to a God who is sovereign.

One time I did a television interview after having written a book. It was one of those horrible things that you don't tell your friends about. I talked more about me than about God. At the end, when I realized what I had done, I decided to say something nice about Jesus, but it was too late—they were rolling the credits.

It wasn't a totally wasted interview, however. At the end the camera crew, the director, and some other people on the staff were sitting around and they started asking me questions. As the discussion went on and on, more and more of the crew had to go back to their jobs, and finally only the director and I were left. Then I remembered I was late for another appointment and said, "I'm late! I've got to go." Then I added, "Tell you what: Let me write down the names of two or three books. If you will read these books, we'll get together again and talk about them."

So I handed him the card and he said, "Thanks a lot." I headed for the door—even now I can close my eyes and see the big swinging door in that studio—and just as I started out the door, he said, "Hey, Reverend." I turned around, and he said, "I'm not going to read these books."

I said, "What do you mean, you 'aren't going to read these books'? You were the one asking all the questions."

He said, "If I read these books, I may find out that you are right. And if you are right, I have to change . . . and I don't want to change."

I had found an honest man! At least he didn't give me any of the nonsense about intellectual questions. He simply said, "I want to be in control; I don't want God to be in control."

One time Larry King and I were having lunch and he was asking questions. I said, "Larry, if I could prove to you beyond a shadow of a doubt that the Christian faith is true, and you would agree that I had won the argument and the facts were true, would you then announce on your radio show that you had become a Christian? Or are you just asking questions because you like to ask questions?"

He said, "Nobody ever asked me that. I'll get back to you."

He never did.

It is a shame that pagans don't accept God's control. But now let's meddle. Let me give you some statements typically made by *Christians* who don't really accept God's control. Have you ever said any of these things:

- "God limits His knowing power, so that I can have perfect freedom."

- "God chooses to save everyone, but we have to choose Him in order to be one of the elect."

- "Don't blame it on God."

- "The Lord votes for you; the Devil votes against you; and you cast the deciding vote."

- "God will not force Himself into anyone's life."

- "God will not interfere in my decisions."

Now, some of those statements do contain a grain of truth. But if you tend to say such things without any qualifiers, it may point to a desire to maintain personal autonomy apart from God. One of my favorite illustrations of God's sovereignty has to do with the character Jill, in *The Silver Chair*, another book in Lewis's Chronicles of Narnia series. If you have read the Chronicles, you know that, like so many other children's books, they are really for adults. You will also recall that Aslan is not a tame lion. He is very big and his growl is very deep. But he loves to play with the kids and they love to hold on to his mane. As we pick up the story in *The Silver Chair*, Jill has ventured into Narnia for the first time. She is very thirsty. She notices a stream of crystal-clear cold water, and then she notices that Aslan is standing between her and the water. Thirsty but afraid, she says to the lion,

> "May I—could I—would you mind going away while I [get a drink of water]?"
>
> The Lion answered this only by a look and a very low growl. And as Jill gazed at its motionless bulk, she realised that she might as well have asked the whole mountain to move aside for her convenience.
>
> The delicious rippling noise of the stream was driving her nearly frantic.
>
> "Will you promise not to—do anything to me, if I do come?" said Jill.
>
> "I make no promise," said the Lion.
>
> Jill was so thirsty now that, without noticing it, she had come a step nearer.
>
> "Do you eat girls?" she said.
>
> "I have swallowed up girls and boys, women and men, kings and emperors, cities and realms," said the Lion. It didn't say this as if it were boasting, nor as if it were sorry, nor as if it were angry. It just said it.
>
> "I daren't come and drink," said Jill.
>
> "Then you will die of thirst," said the Lion.
>
> "Oh dear!" said Jill, coming another step nearer. "I suppose I must go and look for another stream then."
>
> "There is no other stream," said the Lion.[5]

Now, that is the real God. If you don't like the circumstances, don't get mad at other people or at the circumstances, get mad at God! You are not in charge—God is. That is a hard thing to accept, but it is the key to freedom.

Leighton Ford tells about being part of a quartet that sang, "Let's turn the tide for God." Let me tell you something: Where you are right now is where God has ordained you to be right now. Are you willing to recognize the fact that you are not in control of anything? Whenever something bad happens to us, we always get mad at people. Don't get mad at people, get mad at God! He is ultimately responsible for everything.

You can't be free until you are secure. And you can't be secure unless you know the sovereign God who is ruling this whole show.

You Can Count on God

The second bit of theology we need to learn—the second biblical key to our freedom—has to do with the *stability* of God. *God is always the same and you can count on Him.* For you theologians, this is called *immutability*:

For I am the LORD, I do not change. (Malachi 3:6)

Jesus Christ is the same yesterday, today, and forever. (Hebrews 13:8)

Don't you hate change? I do. And if you live in a world where it seems the only thing that doesn't change is change itself, then you have a serious problem.

As you get older, almost everything changes. Did you hear about the three elderly ladies, Gertrude, Gwen, and Sadie, who lived together? Gwen was coming down the stairs one day and Gertrude was in the bathroom. Gertrude called out, "Gwen!"

Gwen said, "Yes, what is it?"

Gertrude said, "Am I getting out of the bathtub or am I getting into the bathtub?"

Gwen said, "You're getting out of the bathtub."

Then Sadie came down the stairs behind Gwen and said, "Gwen, am I going up the stairs or down the stairs?"

Gwen said, "You are going down the stairs."

As Gwen came into the living room, she shook her head and sighed, "Boy, I sure hope I don't ever get to be like Gertrude and Sadie . . . knock on wood! . . . Is that the front door or the back door?"

We all tend to be afraid of change, especially as we grow older. When my father died, I thought I was going to die. Then my brother died. He was my best friend. And then my mother died, and I thought, "Lord, they're all in heaven and I'm the only one left."

I hate change. A friend I write to periodically is in her eighties. She likes to say that she "has a sixteen-year-old soul in an eighty-year-old body." During the sixties, I wrote a couple of books, known mainly for the fact that they didn't sell. One was called, *So Now You Are a Christian*. My target audience was the many young people who were becoming involved in the "Jesus Movement." A couple of years ago, the publisher decided to reissue the book, and they wanted me to write a new introduction. Here is an excerpt from that introduction:

> Someone has said that if you have too many books in your library, the best way to deal with the problem is to take every science book that is more than ten years old and throw it away. I wrote this book nearly two decades ago and there have been a lot a changes in my life since then. On the jacket of the first edition of this book was a photo of the author. Now, as I look at that photo, I wonder what happened to his hair and youthful smile. You wouldn't recognize him now. He's a lot older . . . there are more lines in his face and he doesn't look so young anymore.
>
> The daughters of the young man in the picture are both college graduates and living lives of their own. They are young Christian women whose two fathers (the earthly one and the heavenly one) are proud. Over the years, the young man in that picture has experienced the dramatic loss of his father and his "kid" brother and he has seen the "homegoing" of a lot of his friends.
>
> I look at the picture of the young man on the jacket of that book and I think, *Steve, you were so young then . . . your dreams*

were so big. Nothing was impossible. You were going to win the world to Christ.

A lot has happened since then. He has learned to face the tragedy of unfulfilled dreams and unrealistic expectations. He's learned that he's not as righteous or as knowledgeable as he thought he was.

I look at the picture of the young man and think of the full years of ministry. He has buried more babies and cleaned up after more suicides than he can remember. He has stood beside more deathbeds than most doctors and listened to more confessions than a district attorney. Over the years he has shared more heartbreak and hurt in God's family than he could have known existed. He has had to work hard at not becoming cynical about people or about himself.

When I look at the picture of the young man, I remember that he was whole. The armor has chinks in it now, and because his heart has been broken so many times over the years, he has learned to love more and maybe question more.

But that sounds so bleak.

It hasn't all been that way—not by any means. As I think of that young man, and the years that have passed, I remember his life has been good . . . far better than he ever deserved. A lot of the lines in his face are laugh lines. He is older now and his prayer is still that he "get home before the dark." As the years have passed, he has become more at ease with himself and less concerned about what people will say and think of him.

So many changes.

But some things never change. That young man still has the same wife and he still loves her. She hasn't changed much and sometimes people ask for her father when they are looking for him. But even more important than that . . . God hasn't changed.

That's why there was no need to make many changes in this book. Truth is still truth and the eternal verities are still the same. The truth in this book has gone through a lot of years of testing by the young man on the jacket of the first one.

Jesus is more real to him now than even then.

Throw your science books away. There have been too many changes and they are no longer relevant. But you can keep this one . . . not because it is great but because it is true.

As a longtime member of the family of Christ, the writer
of the first edition of this book is still "trucking." God is still
faithful, and "Jesus Christ is the same yesterday and today
and for ever." (Hebrews 13:8)[6]

When we find ourselves in prison, it is usually because
someone has changed the rules. One of the keys to freedom
is to recognize that God doesn't ever change. His nature is
always the same. His truth is always the same. His
faithfulness is always the same. That is a key to freedom.

God Really Isn't Mad at You!

That brings us to our third theological key to freedom:
God is love, and He really isn't mad at you! John, the disciple
Jesus was perhaps closest to, has this to say about God's
love:

Beloved, let us love one another, for love is of God; and
everyone who loves is born of God and knows God. He who
does not love does not know God, for God is love. (1 John
4:7–8)

Psychologist Karen Horney sees a difference between
"father love" and "mother love." According to her
definitions, father love says, "If you do whatever I want you
to do, then I'll love you," while mother love says, "Whatever
you do, I will love you." That's what God's love is like.

While in Pittsburgh for a speaking engagement a number
of years ago, I was watching television in my hotel room.
Usually, while in my room before speaking, I pray and fast
(and if you believe that, you will believe anything!), but I
was tired of praying and fasting so I turned on the television.
A woman was giving her testimony on one of those religious
programs. She was crying. One doesn't often see people cry
on television, so I kept watching.

As best I can reconstruct it, this is the testimony she gave:

She said she grew up as an atheist and had never been to church, except for one time when she toured a cathedral in Europe. She had never read the Bible and never even prayed a child's prayer like, "Now I lay me down to sleep." She was in her thirties when her daughter was hit by an automobile and left in a coma. She went to the attending physician and asked, "What is the prognosis?"

He said, "It is not good. She could remain in a coma for years, or she could die tomorrow. It is not very good."

The woman said she then walked across the street to a bar, got plastered, and got in her car and drove home. It was raining and she could see the raindrops being wiped away by the windshield wiper. She drove into the driveway of her home, turned the engine off, and began to curse God.

"And I'll tell you something," she said, "I knew how to curse!"

Then, after about a half-hour of spewing out all this venom, she was totally spent and there was silence. And in the silence there was a voice. And the voice said, "That was the first time you ever spoke to Me. And I love you."

Total, unconditional love. You have to understand that about God: total, unconditional love. I don't want you to think that I am antinomian when I say this, but, if you go out tonight, get drunk, drive recklessly and kill someone, God is not going to love you any less than He loves you right now. And if you pray and fast and go to church three times a week and give 40 percent of your income to God's work, He is not going to love you more than He does right now.

As I have mentioned, I grew up with a great fear of abandonment. There were times when my mother tried to leave and I held on to her skirt and begged her to stay because I didn't have anyone but my mother and my brother and he was smaller than I was. So I grew up with an unbelievable fear of abandonment. But God told me that He would never leave me and He would never let me go. Deuteronomy 31:6 says this:

Be strong and of good courage, do not fear nor be afraid of
them; for the LORD your God, He is the One who goes with
you. He will not leave you nor forsake you.

God Guides Us with His Law

Here's the fourth theological key to freedom: *God's Law is
His practical way of teaching and guiding us.* And for the
Christian, that's *all* the Law is.

Oh, how I love Your law!
It is my meditation all the day. (Psalm 119:97)

The function of God's Law for a Christian is quite
different than for a pagan. Now, you need to remember that
the Ten Commandments are not the "Ten Suggestions." And
God intended His commandments to be observed by pagans
as well as by those who believe in Him. The Law was
intended, in part, to keep pagans in line so that the rest of us
could live somewhat normal lives. Some say that the Law
was eliminated when Jesus came. That is absolutely not true:

Do not think that I came to destroy the Law or the Prophets. I
did not come to destroy but to fulfill. For assuredly, I say to
you, till heaven and earth pass away, one jot or one tittle will
by no means pass from the law till all is fulfilled. Whoever
therefore breaks one of the least of these commandments, and
teaches men so, shall be called least in the kingdom of heaven;
but whoever does and teaches them, he shall be called great in
the kingdom of heaven. (Matthew 5:17–19)

The Law never changes. God hasn't changed His ideas
about the Law. But listen to me—this is going to help you:
The purpose of the Law *does* change once you know Christ—
because Christ fulfilled all of the demands of the Law so that
you wouldn't have to.

There's a story told about a man who went to heaven. He

got to the gate and St. Peter said, "You know, you need a thousand points to get in here."

The man said, "I've been going to church all my life and nobody ever told me that!"

St. Peter said, "I don't care, you must have a thousand points to get in here."

The man said, "How do I earn points? By doing good things?"

St. Peter said, "What have you done to earn your points?"

The man said, "Well, I grew up in a Christian home and I went to Sunday school every Sunday for years. In fact, I have a string of Sunday school medals that go to the floor. When I got older, I went to a Christian school and then to a Christian college. Then I went on to graduate school and became a banker. I have always been supportive of the church. I cared about the church all of my life—supported my pastor when others didn't."

He said, "I supported missionaries. As a banker, I cared about my community. I wrote low-income mortgages. I gave loans to people who were in desperate need, and I often gave out of my own pocket. At first I gave 10 percent of my income to God, but as I became more affluent I was giving almost 70 percent."

The man went on, making his case before St. Peter: "I had three children—two boys and a girl. One of my boys is a preacher and the other is a missionary. My girl is married to a missionary in a Third World country.

"I always went to church Sunday morning, Sunday evening, and Wednesday night. Not only that, I worked with the Salvation Army. I rang the bell at Christmas—when it was really cold. And not only did I support missionaries with my money, I went *to* the mission field and supported them with my encouragement."

Then he turned to Peter and said, "How am I doing?"

St. Peter said, "That's one point. What else have you done?"

The man said, "Good Lord, have mercy!"

St. Peter said, "You've got it! Come on in."

You see, the Law has been completely fulfilled in Christ, and mercy has been mediated to us because of what He did on the Cross. God doesn't say to you, "Now that you are a Christian, I will wipe the slate clean." God doesn't give you a fresh slate. He throws the slate away! Forever! He doesn't deal with you on the basis of your goodness or your badness, but on the basis of Christ's finished work on the Cross.

You say, "Then what role does the Law play in a Christian's life? I mean, why do we even have the Law?" Let me answer that question with an acrostic. Let's use the word *R U L E* to discover four ways that the Law is relevant to Christians.

First, the Law *reveals*. It reveals God's will:

You are near, O LORD,
And all Your commandments are truth.
Concerning Your testimonies,
I have known of old that You have founded them forever.
(Psalm 119:151–152)

When my daughters were growing up, I let them know that I would never reject them. But I also wanted them to know what kinds of behavior pleased or displeased me. And I'm glad that God has let me know the way He wants me to live.

Second, the Law *updates*. It keeps you up-to-date on how you are doing in your walk with God:

For the righteous God tests the hearts and minds. (Psalm 7:9)

You have tested my heart;
You have visited me in the night.
You have tried me and have found nothing;
I have purposed that my mouth shall not transgress. (Psalm 17:3)

God tests you for your benefit, not for His benefit. We think He is testing us so that He can find out how we are doing. He *knows* how we are doing! He is testing you for your benefit.

One of my college professors once passed out an exam and then said, "I don't want you to send in your papers and have me grade them. I want you to grade them yourselves, so that you will know how you are doing."

I want to be obedient to God more than any man you have ever met. And I can know how I'm doing by measuring it against His Law.

Third, the Law *lectures:*

> Therefore the law was our tutor to bring us to Christ, that we might be justified by faith. (Galatians 3:24)

The Law is a teacher that brings me to Christ initially, and then keeps me there after I have come to know Him. It doesn't keep me there by my faithfulness, but by my failure. The Christian church is the only organization in the world where the only qualification for membership is that you are not qualified. It is very important to understand that God holds us by His grace. When I look at the Law and measure myself by it and don't live up to it, it scares me to death; and I run to the throne of grace; and that is the purpose of the Law. It teaches me. Before I was a Christian, the Law taught me to feel guilty and I ran to the Cross. Now that I am a Christian, the Law teaches me to stay at the foot of the Cross, receiving His mercy.

Fourth and finally, the Law *educates:*

> Oh, how I love Your law!
> It is my meditation all the day.
> You, through Your commandments,
>   make me wiser than my enemies. (Psalm 119:97–98)

Did you hear about the three clergymen fishing on the boat? The first clergyman got off the boat, saying, "I forgot my lunch" . . . and he proceeded to walk across the water and get his lunch pail.

The second clergyman said, "I forgot a piece of bait. I need to go back." He got off the boat and walked across the water and came back with the bait.

The third pastor looked at these two men and said, "If they can do it, I can too." He said, "Guys, I'll be back in a minute," and he stepped off the boat, went right down, and almost drowned.

The first clergyman said to the second clergyman, "Do you think we ought to tell him where the rocks are?"

God's Law tells you where the rocks are. Better yet, it tells you where the minefields are! Christians should be safer, healthier, happier, and more successful than pagans simply because they know how the world operates. Economist Max Weber has shown that the economic progress that took place in Europe after the Reformation was largely a result of the "Protestant work ethic" inspired by the Reformation. Why? Because the Law of God taught people that they should work.

If you are a Christian, those four things sum up the present purpose of God's Law in your life. It reveals, updates, lectures, and educates. Those are the purposes of the Law for your life, period. If you try to get the Law to save you; if you use it to judge yourself or others; if you use it as a basis for self-righteousness, it will destroy you.

God's Grace Is Far Bigger Than You Can Imagine

The fourth biblical key to freedom had to do with law; key number five has to do with grace: *God's grace is far bigger than you can possibly imagine.* The Israelites had a tangible proof of God's grace toward their nation:

> I have given you a land for which you did not labor, and cities which you did not build, and you dwell in them; you eat of the vineyards and olive groves which you did not plant. (Joshua 24:13)

But the full extent of God's grace was revealed through Christ:

> For by grace you have been saved through faith, and that not of yourselves; it is the gift of God, not of works, lest anyone should boast. (Ephesians 2:8–9)

> Let us therefore come boldly to the throne of grace, that we may obtain mercy and find grace to help in time of need. (Hebrews 4:16)

Early in my seminary teaching, when I was an adjunct professor at Reformed Seminary, I would have full classes—but not because of my ability as a teacher. At the beginning of the term I would tell the class, "I'm not your mother and I'm not interested in your academic standing. I have come here to teach you how to talk. If you listen to and apply what I teach, it will help you. If you don't, it won't. Nevertheless, I'm going to give all of you an automatic *A*. But that doesn't matter. The real exam will come when you step into the pulpit in your church. That is what counts."

So the classes were filled because, no matter how they did, they got an *A*.

God does that. He has given you an *A*. No matter what you do, you have an *A*. It is already decided.

What is grace? Grace is God's unmerited favor to sinful people.

It is important that we understand grace. One time our daughter Robin took a very difficult course in English literature. She sat there on the first day of class and thought, "I'm going to fail this class. I can't do this work. These people know a lot more than I do." She came home to me—and you need to know that daughters get what they want from fathers—and she began to cry and said, "Dad, can I get out of that class and take a regular English course?"

I said, "Of course you can."

So I took her down to the school and we went to the head of the English department, who was a Jewish lady and a wonderful teacher. She looked up and saw me standing there by my daughter, and it looked very certain that Robin was going to cry. There were some students standing around the teacher's desk. She ran them off, saying, "I want to talk to these people." She got the door shut before Robin began to cry.

I said, "I am here to get my daughter out of that English class. It is too difficult for her. The problem with my daughter is that she is too conscientious. So I want you to put her in a regular English class."

She said, "Mr Brown, I understand." Then she looked at Robin and said, "Can I talk to your daughter for a second?"

I said, "Sure."

She said, "Robin, I know how you feel. It is sort of scary sometimes. What if I promised you an A no matter what you did in the class? If I gave you an A before you even started, would you be willing to take the class?"

My daughter is not dumb! She started sniffing and said, "Well, I think I could do that."

The teacher said, "I am going to give you an A in the class. You already have an A, so you go on to the class."

Later, the teacher explained to me what she had done. She said, "I took away the threat of a bad grade, so that she could learn English."

Robin made straight *A*'s on her own in that class!

God, in His grace, deals with you just like that.

There was a father whose son had done something that was particularly bad. He sent him to his room without supper. Later, feeling bad, he took the supper up to the boy's room. Later that evening he went into the room and said, "Son, want to go for ice cream?"

While they were at the ice cream parlor he saw an opportunity to teach his son some theology. He said, "Son, you did something bad, and I sent you to your room without supper. I want you to think about that. That is justice. But when I brought your supper up to your room, that was mercy. Right now you are eating ice cream. That is grace."

Every time you eat a meal, listen to a child laugh, laugh at a joke, collect your paycheck, get out of bed, speak a word . . . that is grace. God's grace. People are always coming to me when they go through difficult times and asking if I think God is judging them for some past sin—usually a specific sin. Sometimes God does chasten, but far less than most people think. Usually I say, "If God were judging you for your sin, you would be dead right now!"

God totally accepts you. That is His grace.

God Is Really There

Biblical key number six relates to the *presence* of God. *God is everywhere, in your joy and in your pain.* He cares. He really does:

> You will show me the path of life;
> In Your presence is fullness of joy;
> At Your right hand are pleasures forevermore. (Psalm 16:11)

I have discovered this through my experience with prayer. One time a number of years ago, I got on my knees. I wasn't trying to make a deal, I just said, "Lord, You are not very real to me. In fact, my sin is more real to me than You are right now. But I'm not going to go to books, or anything else, for an answer; I'm just going to stay here until You become real to me. And if You don't, I'll just stay right here, because I've gone too far to get out and once you see truth you can't get out of it. Once you see truth, you can't unsee it. I want to know You in the deepest possible way."

God honored that prayer. And gradually, over the next few years, God became so real to me that sometimes I couldn't believe it. He would come in the silence. I'm not a very spiritual person. I'm not a mystic. But I want you to know that the most important part of my life is my prayer time—not because I have to do it, but because it is a soft place. It is the one place where I can be totally honest, and where I can be accepted.

There are times when I can hardly wait to get away from people, so that I can go before the throne. And there are times when I can honestly say to people, "I have been with the Father this morning"—and *really mean* that I was with the Father this morning.

During the early sixties, when a few theologians began to talk about the "death of God," Billy Graham said, "I know there is a God. I talked with Him this morning."

One of my professors at Boston University said, "That is not the issue; the issue is, did He speak back?"

As we come to the close of our look at how God's nature makes us free, let's talk a little more about prayer. I don't think you can really get free from a prison until you learn about the soft place of prayer. Too many of us are praying because we feel like we ought to, or because the preacher told us we should. We are not praying for the right reasons.

So here's our mini-course in prayer:

S I L E N C E: Finding Freedom in Prayer

When you are talking about real prayer, systems don't work. A lawyer friend of mine decided that he wanted to know how to pray. He told me he read a book on prayer, and said to himself, "Now I know what I've been doing wrong. It is just a matter of following the rules. You follow the rules and prayer is good."

He said, "So I followed all the rules in the book, and it was the worst time of prayer I have ever had in my life."

Now, I don't want you to junk everything you know about prayer. A lot of stuff you have learned is good. It's just not good enough. I'm going to say some things that most folks don't say, so stay with me. I'm going to do it with another acrostic. The acrostic is S I L E N C E.

First, freeing prayer is prayed out of *stillness*:

Be still, and know that I am God. (Psalm 46:10)

The famous pianist Artur Rubinstein once got hoarse at a time when he had been reading a *Reader's Digest* article on cancer, and therefore decided that he had cancer of the throat. He went to the doctor and said, "I'm grown and I have lived a full life and I can take the bad news, so tell me the truth."

The doctor said, "Your only problem is that you have been talking too much."

We evangelicals have been talking too much. We have overlooked our need for silence. Why pray, if God already knows what you are going to say? I mean, why ask Him for stuff that He already knows you want? Why confess sins that He already knows you have committed? Have you ever watched two lovers in a restaurant just holding hands and looking at each other? That's what prayer is. You don't have to wax eloquent before God. Just be still.

Some of the best praying I have ever done has taken

place *after* I have prayed—when God has said, "Quit blithering and just be still." If you really want prayer to make a difference, then learn to be silent. Basil Pennington, in his book, *Centered Living: The Way of Centering Prayer*,[7] says that life is sort of like a river, and when you pray, you climb out of the river. The boats, the barges, and all the flotsam of life keep on going down the river, while you sit on the side, center in on prayer, and let the river go. You learn to let the time go by without having to say very much.

Second, freeing prayer uses *imagination*. That is the *I* in *S I L E N C E*. The prophet Joel talks about imagination:

> And it shall come to pass afterward
> That I will pour out My Spirit on all flesh;
> Your sons and your daughters shall prophesy,
> Your old men shall dream dreams,
> Your young men shall see visions. (Joel 2:28)

One thing that really ticks me off about the "New Age" movement is that they have tried to steal some very good biblical concepts and symbols—such as the rainbow. I love rainbows, but you can't even have a rainbow in a painting without some fellow Christian suspecting you of being a New Ager.

They have done that with prayer. Don't be afraid to use your imagination in prayer. If you really want to be a part of the New Age or of some Eastern religion, then try to make your mind totally blank when you pray. But if you're a Christian, don't be afraid to use your imagination. Sometimes when I pray, I will picture myself walking with Christ in one of the biblical settings. I don't know James Robison, except to see him occasionally on television, but he said something the other day that I thought was great. He said that, after he repented and went back to God to pray, God said, "I'm glad you came here, James, not many people come here anymore."

Let me tell you something else I do to use my imagination in prayer. There is a wonderful chapel at a monastery in Conyers, Georgia, and sometimes when I pray, I picture myself kneeling in that chapel, and Christ is the altar. I picture all the people I pray for, which amounts to two or three hundred each morning. We are all sitting in the congregation in that chapel, and Jesus is up front. Instead of telling Jesus what they need, I mentally go to each of those people, take them by the hand, walk them up front, and give them to Jesus. When I started doing that, it was amazing how many people on my prayer list told me that God was becoming more real to them!

Third, freeing prayer is *listening* prayer:

Therefore Eli said to Samuel, "Go, lie down; and it shall be, if He calls you, that you must say, 'Speak, LORD, for Your servant hears.'" So Samuel went and lay down in his place. Now the LORD came and stood and called as other times, "Samuel! Samuel!" And Samuel answered, "Speak, for Your servant hears." Then the Lord said to Samuel . . . (1 Samuel 3:9–11)

Sherwood Wirt wrote a wonderful book titled *Not Me, God*.[8] It is about a man who, while shaving one morning, cuts himself and says, "Oh, God." And God says, "Yes? What is it?" The rest of the book is a conversation between the man and God. It is a wonderful little book. We sometimes think that God doesn't speak anymore. He does speak, but you have to listen. Try writing down your thoughts as you pray. You will soon realize that many of those thoughts come directly from God. The problem is, we are too busy to listen—we just want to talk.

Fourthly, freeing prayer is *eulogistic*. That comes from the Greek *eulogeo*, meaning to praise:

Enter into His gates with thanksgiving,
And into His courts with praise. (Psalm 100:4)

You want a cheap high? Next time you pray, just praise God. Don't do anything, don't ask Him for anything, just tell Him how wonderful He is. I mean, just praise God. You will find yourself ushered into the throne room. I don't subscribe to all of what is generally described as "charismatic" doctrine, but sometimes I go to charismatic services simply because charismatics do a lot of praising. I can sense God's presence in the praise. Let me give you two dynamite verses:

But You are holy,
Enthroned in the praises of Israel. (Psalm 22:3)

Now the Lord is the spirit; and where the Spirit of the Lord is, there is liberty. (2 Corinthians 3:17)

Put those two verses together and you have a "prayer process for freedom": (1) Praise brings the Spirit of God; (2) the Spirit of God brings freedom.

Paul says we are to praise God in everything. The secret of freedom is relinquishment. And relinquishment is just another of way of saying, whatever it is, it is from God, and I will praise Him for it. One of our daughters used to have a poster of Ziggy standing on a mountain top at sunrise. He is jumping up and down, and the caption says, "Yea, God!"

Learn to say, "Yea, God" in your prayers, and see what happens.

Fifth, freeing prayer is *natural*. In Psalm 139, as King David is talking to the Lord, he says,

I hate them with perfect hatred;
I count them my enemies. (verse 22)

Now, that messes up a wonderful and comforting psalm, doesn't it! What is going on? What is going on is that the

Psalms are not theological tomes, they are honest expressions of honest people, pouring out their hearts to a loving God. Don't tell God you love Him if you don't. St. Theresa once said, "Lord, You would have more friends if You would treat the ones You have better."

Some folks are shocked by such a bold statement, but they shouldn't be. Whenever you read the great contemplatives, they are honest before God. If you don't love God; if you aren't repentant; if you don't want to serve Him, for God's sake don't lie to Him. Let your prayer be natural and normal. Tell Him what you really think.

Next comes *confession.* Freeing prayer goes to God with honest confession:

> If we confess our sin, He is faithful and just to forgive us our sins and to cleanse us from all unrighteousness. (1 John 1:9)

Confession is a child of God agreeing with the judgment of God. Confession frees you up like nothing else will. Go to your heavenly Father and confess—and He will hug you.

Finally, freeing prayer is *enigmatic.* The prayer that frees us from our prisons does not have to be a prayer we fully understand:

> "For My thoughts are not your thoughts,
> Nor are your ways My ways," says the LORD.
> "For as the heavens are higher than the earth,
> So are My ways higher than your ways,
> And My thoughts than your thoughts." (Isaiah 55:8)

Several years ago, Anna made me a banner that declared, "My Father, I don't understand You, but I trust You." One of the greatest hindrances to real freedom is the need to understand. Anything you can explain, you can control. If you can control God, He is not God—you are. The older I get, the less I understand God and the more I love Him.

The essence of Christian maturity is a high tolerance for ambiguity. A number of years ago, a leader of a large denomination received a lot of publicity by saying that God didn't hear the prayers of unbelievers and especially Jews. Well, let me tell you something: When you go to God, remember that He is God and He can do whatever He wants to do and think whatever He wants to think . . . and you will never understand. You are there to serve and to worship God, not to understand Him.

When you know God the way He wants to be known, the way He has revealed Himself, it will bring you freedom.

7

Sixteen Principles to Help You Be Free

In Proverbs 1:5 we read,

> A wise man will hear and increase learning,
> And a man of understanding will obtain wise counsel.

In this chapter we will explore sixteen biblical "power principles" that will help you break free from prison, whether it be one of the prisons we listed at the outset—sin, guilt, failure, the past, self-abasement, perfectionism, fear, needing approval, obligation, rules, religion, and gurus—or some other prison you are in right now. You'll probably find this to be the only chapter in the whole book that doesn't follow any logical system. These are just some things I've learned that I think could make a difference in your life. These are some of the building blocks we can use to tear down our prisons and build a house of joy.

So let's dig in.

Nothing Is Fair, Nothing Is Perfect . . .

The first power principle is this: *Nothing lasts, nothing is fair, nothing is perfect, and you aren't home yet.* Jesus said,

These things I have spoken to you, that in Me you may have peace. In the world you will have tribulation; but be of good cheer, I have overcome the world. (John 16:33)

One of the great hindrances to Christian freedom is false expectations, the feeling that there is something magical about the Christian faith which will make the fallen world unfallen. Such thinking is the bane of Christian freedom.

One of the very few good things about our daughters being married and no longer living at home is the fact that every stray animal that comes into our yard no longer gets fed. There was a time when we had twelve or thirteen cats because one of our daughters thought it was the Christian thing to feed a very prolific mother cat. I asked the vet, once these cats started multiplying, what was I going to do about them? He said, "Did you feed them?" I said, "My daughter did." And he said, "They're yours!"

Now, one of the problems with feeding all those cats in your back yard is that you end up feeding every other wild animal in the neighborhood. We fed snakes and foxes and rats and, most of all, we ended up feeding the entire raccoon population of southern Florida. One evening I heard some noise in the back yard. When I looked, I saw a raccoon sitting on the yard table eating the food we had put there for the cats. It irritated me and I decided to fix the problem once and for all. I got out a high-powered hose and gave him a shot he is probably still feeling. He ran down the side of the yard and I figured that was it. Then five minutes later I heard a noise and that sucker was back on the table eating the food. I hosed him down again and he ran again, but this time not quite as far.

After five hosings he didn't run anymore. In fact he stood up on the table, with his arms outstretched toward me as if to say, "Go ahead, do it to me again. And when you're tired, I'm going to eat this food."

What happened to that raccoon is what ought to happen to a Christian living in a fallen world. If you think things are going to work out, you are crazy. If you believe that your ship is going to come in, you will believe anything. If you expect that luck is going to smile on you all the time, and everything is going to be fine, you are living in a dream world.

Paul Harvey once said that he and his wife decided they were going cancel Christmas, because absolutely nothing could live up to those kinds of expectations. Not every problem has a solution. You can't clean up every mess you make. You can't put toothpaste back into the tube. If your expectations go beyond what one should expect in a fallen world, not only will you be disappointed, but you will think that the reason things don't go according to expectation is that you have done something wrong.

And that brings me to an important "sub-principle": Most painful experiences you endure do not result from God's judgment. His grace is bigger than that. I have a friend who committed adultery, twenty years before she confessed it to me. I was the only one she had ever told. After a lot of discussion and prayer we decided, in her case—and each case is individual—that she should tell her husband. The next day I saw her and she looked like a little girl. In fact, she was giggling. I asked her what had happened.

She replied, "He told me that he had known it all these years and had forgiven me from the beginning. He said, 'I wondered if you would ever come to me with it.'"

The interesting thing about my friend is that every bad thing she had experienced in all those years she had thought was God's judgment on her sin. That was a lie. Her husband, and God, had forgiven her. There is no punishment for forgiven sin, or it isn't forgiven.

There is a Jessica Fletcher who lives on Key Biscayne. She likes to say, "The only difference between me and the Jessica Fletcher on TV is that if you invite me to dinner one of your guests is not going to die." Sometimes we assume that, because God is a part of our lives, there is a causal relationship between the bad things that happen to us and God's relationship with us. Nothing could be further from the truth. Whether or not you are a Christian, as long as you are human and living in a fallen world, nothing lasts, nothing is fair, nothing is perfect, and you aren't home yet.

People Are What They Want to Be

A second power principle is: *People are what they have decided to be*:

As he thinks in his heart, so is he. (Proverbs 23:7)

Do you want to be made well? (John 5:6)

People often choose destructive patterns of behavior simply because the "payback" or reward for that behavior is greater than the pain it causes. When the pain becomes greater than the payback, creative change starts to take place.

A number of years ago I was counseling a young man who was like the old man in "Li'l Abner"—he walked around with a dark cloud over his head. The young man simply couldn't figure out what he was doing wrong. His business, his family, his whole life was a total mess. Every counseling approach we tried failed. Every creative solution we applied to his problems ended up in disaster. We were sitting and talking one day when I got one of those revelations of truth one sometimes receives about a particular situation. My charismatic friends call it a word of knowledge, and my pagan friends call it insight.

I said to the young man, "Something just dawned on me: You don't really want to fix those problems. The reason the solutions aren't working is because you don't want them to work. So instead of talking about what you can do to change your horrible situation, let's talk about *why you don't want to change* your horrible situation. What is the payback for having your life so messed up?"

At first I thought he was going to kill me. But then he got the same insight. He said, "You know, you may be right."

You know what was happening? He was afraid to try to succeed, because he might fail. It was easier for him unconsciously to say that his life was falling apart because of uncontrollable circumstances. What was the payback? He received a lot of sympathy for his problems, instead of the condemnation he thought would follow his certain failure.

We also discovered that he was a perfectionist. Now, a perfectionist is someone who genuinely believes that there is only one right way to do something, and that as long as you don't do it the wrong way, you still haven't blown your perfection. This young man didn't want the solutions to his problems because none of them were perfect solutions.

What was the payback? Since he hadn't tried a solution and failed, in his mind he was still perfect.

For years I would tell my congregation that I didn't want to be a pastor. I would say, "You leave me alone and I'll leave you alone. I will be your teacher, but not your mother." I used to say that I was a conscript for the job, not a volunteer. I'd say that if the session fired me, I would consider it a favor—then I could go into vinyl repair and do something productive.

One time Fred Smith said, "Steve, do you know what bothers me about you?"

I allowed that I didn't.

He said, "Your problem is that you carry around a portable foxhole—with all this talk about not wanting to be a pastor. That way, if you fail, you can say that you didn't want to do it in the first place."

I thought about it and decided he was right. Not only that, I discovered that I had followed that pattern in many areas of my life. For instance, when I was a student in high school, I graduated third from the bottom. The teachers couldn't understand it, because I had tested so high on an IQ test. I would always say, "I hate school and I'm not going to try." What was the payback? If I failed by not trying it was a whole lot better to my self-image than to try hard and then fail.

Now, I want you to clearly understand what I am saying about this particular power principle. I'm not giving you the nonsense that you will receive from the New Age movement—that you can become whatever you think you can become, simply by using your imagination. I'm not saying that you can will away cancer or a cold. I'm not saying that you can think your way out of every problem. What I am saying is this: Most Christians are depressed because they have decided to be depressed. Most Christians are not free because they have decided not to be free. Most Christians allow others to control their lives because they *want* others to control their lives. Most Christians feel guilty all the time because they have decided to feel guilty all the time.

Let me ask you some questions:

• Where do you get your emotional payback for destructive behavior? Answer that question and you will stop the destructive behavior.

• Where are you failing in your life right now because you think you deserve failure? Answer that question and you will quit failing.

• Where are you allowing others to control you because it is easier to be irresponsible? Answer that question and you will stop allowing others to control you.

• Why do you put people on a pedestal? Answer that question and you will quit doing it.

• Why do you find it hard to say no? Because you think people like you more when you say yes? Because you are insecure? Because you are afraid? Find out what the payback is and you will learn to say no.

Later on, I'll be suggesting some very practical ways to establish your freedom in Christ. I want to create a "fellowship of the free" all over the country. Some of you, I suspect, are going to say, "I just can't! I just can't! I want to be part of the fellowship of the free, but I just can't."

If you are not a part of it, it will be because you did not *want* to be a part of it. When you find out why you don't want to be free, then you will be free. Why? Because when the pain is greater than the payback, change takes place.

Sickness Comes from Trying to Avoid Pain!

Our third power principle is this: *Almost all emotional and spiritual sickness comes from an inappropriate effort to avoid pain.* No one could possibly accuse Jesus of promising His followers a rose garden:

> When He had called the people to Himself, with His disciples also, He said to them, "Whoever desires to come after Me, let him deny himself, and take up his cross, and follow Me. For whoever desires to save his life will lose it, but whoever loses his life for My sake and the gospel's will save it. For what will it profit a man if he gains the whole world, and loses his own soul? Or what will a man give in exchange for his soul?" (Mark 8:34–37)

In fact, rose gardens are pretty rare in the Bible:

> My son, do not despise the chastening of the LORD,
> Nor be discouraged when you are rebuked by Him;
> For whom the LORD loves He chastens,
> And scourges every son whom He receives. (Hebrews 12:5–6)

> We also glory in tribulations, knowing that tribulation produces perseverance; and perseverance, character; and character, hope. Now hope does not disappoint, because the love of God has been poured out in our hearts by the Holy Spirit who was given to us. (Romans 5:3–5)

A great theologian and philosopher, Mary Tyler Moore, once said, "If it doesn't hurt some, you are doing it wrong." Or to put it in another way, "No pain, no gain." In the earlier years of plastic surgery, it was believed that by using an anesthetic you would hurt the results of the surgery. So one was faced with a decision: Suffer and become beautiful; or avoid suffering and remain ugly. In the last section we talked about the payback for staying in your prison—the false comfort and affirmation and security "enjoyed" by those who never try. Now let's talk about the pain that can be involved in breaking out of prison.

To be quite honest, if you are free, not everyone will like you. If you are free, you will sometimes feel insecure. If you say no, you will sometimes feel guilty. If you are your own person, bowing your head before none but God, you are going to be rejected by a lot of authority figures. One of the problems with most of us is that we have been in the prison for so long that the prison begins to seem normal. When you first start walking in the light, it hurts your eyes. There will be a tendency to think, when your eyes hurt, that you must be doing it wrong. No, no, no! The darkness of the prison won't hurt your eyes, but you can't see anything, either!

Emotional and spiritual sickness comes from an inappropriate effort to avoid pain.

Circumstances Don't Create, They Reveal

The fourth power principle is this: *Time, circumstance, and opportunity do not create good or evil—they only reveal it.* Peter understood this principle. He knew that the time of persecution he saw coming would reveal the authenticity of the faith of many young Christians:

> In this you greatly rejoice, though now for a little while, if need be, you have been grieved by various trials, that the genuineness of your faith, being much more precious than

gold that perishes, though it is tested by fire, may be found to praise, honor, and glory at the revelation of Jesus Christ. (1 Peter 1:6)

Did you hear about the man whose younger colleague was promoted over him? He was quite angry about it and went to the president of the company. He said, "I don't see how you could promote him when he has so little experience. I have twenty-five years of experience."

The president replied, "No, you don't have twenty-five years of experience. You have one year of experience, and you have repeated it twenty-four times."

The circumstance of being passed over for promotion didn't ruin the older man's career, it simply revealed how he had ruined his own career.

Circumstances don't create the evil in our lives. Most Christians walk around like the three proverbial monkeys, trying to avoid seeing evil, hearing evil, or thinking evil, lest they will be tainted by it. But according to Jesus, they've got it all backwards:

Do you not yet understand that whatever enters the mouth goes into the stomach and is eliminated? But those things that proceed out of the mouth come from the heart, and they defile a man. For out of the heart proceed evil thoughts, murders, adulteries, fornications, thefts, false witness, blasphemies. These are the things which defile a man, but to eat with unwashed hands does not defile a man. (Matthew 15:17–20)

What is on the inside, Jesus says, will eventually manifest itself on the outside. The evil things Christians try so hard to avoid may already be in their hearts, simply waiting for the right opportunity to come out. Meanwhile, the evil that is on the outside will never get inside—unless we have already made room for it.

Legalism is, by one definition, separating oneself from any known sin. There was once an advertisement for a midwestern Bible college that read, "100 Miles From Any

Known Sin." A Christian can go off and enter a convent or a monastery, and get away from sin. Or the Christian can live a full life, allowing God to teach through the circumstances, leading to growth and change in his or her life. That is what life is all about.

What you do has no bearing on your acceptance by God, but it does reveal who you *are*. The reason Jesus could deal with prostitutes and tax collectors and winos was because He was not a prostitute, tax collector, or wino. The reason you can live a full life without all the taboos that Christians generally put on living is because: If you succeed in being faithful, you will praise God for His grace; and if you fail, you will know how to pray so that *next* time you will succeed and praise Him for His grace.

Circumstances don't create good or evil in our lives— they only reveal the good or evil that is already there.

You Are Your Only Important Enemy

The fifth power principle is this: *The only important battle you will ever fight will be with yourself.* If you don't believe that, just ask Paul. He fought that battle all the time:

> For the good that I will to do, I do not do; but the evil I will not to do, that I practice. . . . O wretched man that I am! Who will deliver me from this body of death? (Romans 7:19, 24)

Jesus knew all about the battle, and knew that most of us spend most of our time fighting the wrong enemy:

> Judge not, that you be not judged. For with what judgment you judge, you will be judged; and with the measure you use, it will be measured back to you. And why do you look at the speck in your brother's eye, but do not consider the plank in your own eye? Or how can you say to your brother, "Let me remove the speck from your eye"; and look, a plank is in your own eye? Hypocrite! First remove the plank from your own

eye, and then you will see clearly to remove the speck from your brother's eye. (Matthew 7:1–5)

I am not your mother. And you are not my mother. That means that I am not responsible for your obedience and you are not responsible for mine. You are responsible for your own obedience and I'm responsible for mine.

Upon first accepting the call to be a pastor in Miami, I had no idea of all the problems I was getting into. I received more suicide calls my first year in Miami than in all my previous twelve years as a pastor combined. When suicide calls came in I would say, "Look, if you want to take your life, nobody can stop you. It is the most egocentric, selfish, destructive act that can ever happen. If you do it, don't make me a part of it. I am not responsible for your acts. I will mourn. I will be sad. I will grieve at your passing, but I will not be either guilty or responsible."

Hopefully, the person would not hang up until I said something more positive than that. But it is important to establish the ground rules. None of us can spend our whole life feeling guilty for someone else's sin. Nor do other people owe us anything. One of the central foundations of a mature, free, responsible Christian is the understanding that his or her happiness, freedom, and well-being is not dependent on anyone else, on anywhere else, or on any other time period.

A young man came to me with a drug problem. He said he couldn't stop. I said, "What do you mean, you 'can't stop'? Do you mean your friends tie you down and force drugs into your mouth? Do you mean the drug pushers hold a gun to your head and tell you that, if you don't buy and use the drugs, they will pull the trigger? Do you mean that others force you into your drug lifestyle?"

He said, "No, not exactly."

"Then why don't you stop?"

He said, "I never thought of it that way."

And he stopped.

Too often, marriages and relationships fail because

people try to garner all of their emotional worth from another person. No one but God can give you emotional worth. We are so critical of others in the church, trying to make them fit into our mold. And even worse, people are so critical of us and we allow it. Stop it! My battle is with myself, and your battle is with yourself.

Only Cows Are Totally Content

And now the sixth power principle to help you find freedom: *The contentment of cows works only for cows.* Or, in the words of John 16:33: "In the world you will have tribulation."

People are always telling me that they "don't feel peace" about something, and that therefore they don't believe it is God's will. I have never felt peace about anything God has told me to do in my whole life! If peace, in the contented cow sense, were the measurement of whether I was in God's will, I have never been in God's will.

I wrote about that in my first book, *Where the Action Is.*[9] More than twenty-five years ago I decided I couldn't play games anymore. I was going to be honest with people about the nonsense. I remember those early days. I couldn't sleep at night. I had bad dreams when I did sleep. Bad dreams of standing naked before the congregation. Or worse, of standing before them in red-polka-dotted underwear. I decided I was going to be honest . . . and it gave me no peace. There is a short-term asset to sin and a long-term liability. There is a short-term liability to righteousness and a long-term pay-off. If we got it all up front, we would never sin and would always act righteously. If you are looking for short-term peace by being free, you are in for quite a shock. If you are looking for a long-term pay-off, you have come to the right place.

Let me tell you the rest of the story: While those early years of ministry were horrible in terms of peace, I can now feel comfortable with myself—because I have never tried to be something I'm not. And that is freedom.

There Are No "Super-Christians"

The seventh power principle that will help you be free is this: *There are no "super-Christians."* If you have found one, you have diminished yourself,

> For all have sinned and fall short of the glory of God. (Romans 3:23)

In a church where I served in Boston, we sometimes had a time of testimony. There was a man who stood up and gave God praise for bringing him into a position of conquering sin. God had removed so much sin from his life, he said, that his eyes welled up with tears whenever he talked about it. Now, let me tell you the truth. He was one of the most critical and mean-spirited Christians I have ever known. He had destroyed his son and was very close to doing the same with his daughter. He was narrow, negative, and nauseating. I almost stood up and said, "You hypocrite! Why don't you tell them the truth? I'm not even sure you are saved."

There was a man in that same congregation who had been a Christian for only two years. He came into my study the day after the testimony meeting and said, "Steve, I'm not coming to church anymore. I just can't be the kind of Christian I ought to be."

I asked him how he had come to that conclusion. He replied, "Last night I listened to Sam talk, and decided I'll never be as good as him."

I told him, "I hope to God that you never are!"

God has allowed me to know and be friends with a lot of very public and well-known evangelical leaders. I spend my whole life looking for heroes, and I have often thought I had found them—until I got to know them. To my horror, I found out that they were just like me—afraid, sinful, and wounded. I really didn't like that at first, but it has become a really wonderful gift. Because we have now become brothers. One of the reasons I don't like the words *discipleship* or *discipling* is that those words imply something that ought not exist in the church. I will be your older friend. I will teach you doctrine, but I will not be your discipler. Only God can be that.

Frank Jean, a Chinese man living in New England, is one of the deepest Christians I know anywhere. He came to America as a missionary. One time when we had lunch together, I said, "Frank, everyone has a pastor except me. I don't have anyone to go to with my sin and pain and hurt. Would you be my pastor?"

I'll never forget his answer. He was eating soup at the time. He put his spoon down and waited a long time before he answered. Then he said, "Steve, I can't be your pastor. Only Jesus can do that for you. I'll be your friend."

Are you afraid? Everybody is. Do you worry about your sin? Everybody does. Are you worried about getting caught? Everybody is. Are you lonely? Everybody is. Have you failed? Everybody does. Of course, if you proclaimed that truth in most churches, people might make you feel like a weirdo. But you are not. You're just a little boy telling the emperor that he doesn't have any clothes. Pretty soon everybody will know it and the church will be healthier for it.

Be Glad When Dogs Play Checkers

Power principle number eight: *When a dog plays checkers, we don't criticize his game.* We are pleased and surprised that he is playing at all. Likewise we should be pleased when fallen human beings do anything good at all:

> For we know that the whole creation groans and labors with birth pangs together until now. Not only that, but we also

who have the firstfruits of the Spirit, even we ourselves groan within ourselves, eagerly waiting for the adoption, the redemption of our body. For we were saved in this hope. (Romans 8:22–24)

Beloved, now we are children of God; and it has not yet been revealed what we shall be, but we know that when He is revealed, we shall be like Him. (1 John 3:2)

Not that I have already attained, or am already perfected; but I press on, that I may lay hold of that for which Christ Jesus has also laid hold of me. Brethren, I do not count myself to have apprehended; but one thing I do, forgetting those things which are behind and reaching forward to those things which are ahead, I press toward the goal for the prize of the upward call of God in Christ Jesus. (Philippians 3:12)

We tend to let our culture creep into our theology. We believe that everything should be instant. In the Christian life, everything happens in a process, and it is a source of great grief when a Christian doesn't recognize that. That is why it is desperately important that we don't have a mold into which all Christians have to fit.

We tend to make the excellent the enemy of the good. And often the good is about all that you can get in this world. Your husband isn't perfectible. Your wife isn't perfectible. Your pastor isn't perfectible. Your church isn't perfectible. And most of all, *you* are not perfectible. Once you accept that, you can accept a lot about yourself and others.

Once when I was a pastor, I made a fool out of myself. I had preached a reasonably good sermon and was standing on the patio after the service, shaking hands. Unknown to me, a man had come to the church during the service and put some slanderous flyers on the windows of hundreds of cars in the parking lot. He had a grievance against one of our members and, not being able to get people to agree with him, decided to get revenge.

While I was standing there saying sweet, spiritual things to people who shook my hand, one of the men in the church brought me one of the flyers and said, "Steve, these were on all the cars in the parking lot."

I lost it! I turned red in the face and uttered a word that I'm sure the young couple standing in front of me had never heard from a clergyman. Before I had realized what I had done, it was too late. I turned to the young couple and said, "I'm so sorry."

The young lady laughed and said, "Dr. Brown, it's nice to know that you are human. I don't feel so intimidated anymore."

How much better off we all would be if we would say to our brothers and sisters, "You know, you did a stupid thing. Welcome to the club! It's nice to know that you are human like me."

Or if we said it to ourselves, "Well, I'm only human."

In *The Goodness of God*,[10] John Wenham reverses the traditional pagan argument about the goodness of God this way: The issue is not, If there is a good God, why is there so much suffering in the world? The issue is, If there is a just God, why is there not *more* suffering in the world? Likewise, the issue is not, If I am a Christian, why do I sin? Rather, the issue is, If I am by nature a sinner, why don't I sin more?

When a dog plays checkers, you don't criticize his game. You are just pleased and surprised that he is playing at all. During one of our preaching classes at the seminary a young man said to me, "Mr. Brown, I want you to be very hard on me, I can take it. Tell me the truth."

I wanted to say, "Son, if I told you how bad your preaching really is, you would go into vinyl repair. But you are just a student and I am pleased that you are doing it at all."

This is not a brief for slovenly living. It is, rather, the facing of an unpleasant truth—that you and your family and your pastor and your church and your friends are not perfectible. The worker who is aware of imperfections will create a more perfect product. Just so, a Christian aware of and accepting of his or her imperfections will become a more perfect Christian.

There Is Power in Weakness

The ninth power principle turns conventional wisdom upside down: *God's power is made perfect in weakness:*

> And lest I should be exalted above measure by the abundance of the revelations, a thorn in the flesh was given to me, a messenger of Satan to buffet me, lest I be exalted above measure. Concerning this thing I pleaded with the Lord three times that it might depart from me. And He said to me, "My grace is sufficient for you, for My strength is made perfect in weakness." (2 Corinthians 12:7–9)

Did you ever notice that the Bible hardly ever says what you think it is going to say. The text I read to you is one of those cases. It ought to read, "God's power is made perfect when you have gotten your own power revved up as high as it can possibly go." But it doesn't say that. It says God's power is made perfect in weakness.

A friend of mine is a friend of Chris Evert, the tennis star. My friend tried to lead her to Christ. She always refused—because, she said, it would take away her competitive edge. That may be true in tennis (though I doubt it). However, even if it is true in tennis, it isn't true in life. Out of our weakness God is able to create strength. The American folk religion says, "God helps those who help themselves." The Bible says, "God helps those who can't help themselves and know it." As you consider the issues raised in this book you will face the reality of admitting your weakness to yourself and maybe even to others. You will see that such admission is an important step to freedom. The world doesn't know it, but that is the great secret of the Christian life.

The servant principles of the Scriptures are very important, because they point the way to how Christians get authority. By *authority*, I mean the appropriate and biblical use of power. You don't get authority from a gun, from political power, or from shouting; you get authority from serving in weakness. I am a sinner. Are you? Doesn't that feel better? I am weak in so many areas, afraid and lonely, and constantly afraid that people will find out that I am not as smart or spiritual or good as they think I am. Once you know that you are weak; once you know that you are not perfect; once you know that you don't have anything by which to commend yourself before God . . . you don't have anything to protect anymore. You don't have to be right anymore. Then you are free. And in that freedom there is tremendous power.

Demons Die in the Light

Power principle number ten is: *Demons die in the light:*

Confess your sins to each other and pray for each other so that you may be healed. (James 5:16 NIV)

O Corinthians! We have spoken openly to you, our heart is wide open. (2 Corinthians 6:11)

For we do not want you to be ignorant, brethren, of our trouble which came to us in Asia: that we were burdened beyond measure, above strength, so that we despaired even of life. (2 Corinthians 1:8)

Behold, You desire truth in the inward parts,
And in the hidden part You will make me to know wisdom.
(Psalm 51:6)

Frederick Buechner, in his book *Telling Secrets*[11], talks about his father's suicide, the unspoken tragedy of his family, and his daughter's anorexia. He said something very profound—that when we tell our secrets, even if only to ourselves, they lose their power.

As I was working on the seminars from which this book is drawn, I took a break and spoke for a conference of some three thousand people. They were some of the straightest, most fundamentalist evangelical Christians in America. Because I had been working on this material, I decided to tell them some of my secrets. It was a big-time risk for me to do so, and I told them that. I talked about my father's alcoholism and my fear of abandonment; about being a second generation bastard; about my grandfather's suicide. I spoke very quietly, certain that after I was finished they would stone me.

You know what happened? As I looked over that auditorium, I noticed that, everywhere, people were quietly weeping. I didn't know what was happening, but after the meeting, I was inundated by honest, loving, and caring people. As soon as I had finished, a man came running down the aisle, and literally picked me up and hugged me. I noticed that he was sobbing. He said, "Oh, brother, my father committed suicide, and I have never told anyone until now."

Another woman told me that she had been diagnosed with cancer and had not even told her husband. "Steve," she said, "I'm afraid to die."

Another woman said, "Steve, I have never told anyone this, but I was sexually abused by my father. And for the first time this morning, I felt there was hope."

When the demons get into the light, they die. What are your demons? Tell your secrets to a friend, and if you can't do that, tell them to yourself. Ask God to reveal your demons. And ask Him to take away the armor.

Dirt Is Fixable, but Stiffness Will Kill You

Here's another freedom-producing power principle: *It is easier to hug a dirty kid than to hug a stiff kid:*

The sacrifices of God are a broken spirit,
A broken and a contrite heart—
These, O God, You will not despise. (Psalm 51:17)

Also He spoke this parable to some who trusted in themselves that they were righteous, and despised others: "Two men went up to the temple to pray, one a Pharisee and the other a tax collector. The Pharisee stood and prayed thus with himself, 'God, I thank You that I am not like other men—extortioners, unjust, adulterers, or even as this tax collector. I fast twice a week; I give tithes of all that I possess.' And the tax collector, standing afar off, would not so much as raise his eyes to heaven, but beat his breast, saying, 'God, be merciful to me a sinner!' I tell you, this man went down to his house justified rather than the other; for everyone who exalts himself will be humbled, and he who humbles himself will be exalted." (Luke 18:9–14)

I was in the study reading one day when Sara, a teenager in the church, opened the door and walked in. She didn't even knock. No respect for the clergy! I put the book down and said, "What is it, Sara?"

She said, "I was at a Bible study last night and I learned something important."

"What did you learn?" I asked.

"I learned that you can't hug a stiff kid."

I thought about that for a moment and decided she was right. You can't. Have you ever tried to hug a sullen teenager? It is like hugging a telephone pole. I told Sara that I would probably use her observation in a sermon sometime. I picked up my book, hoping that she would take the hint and leave. But she didn't, she just stood there smiling. I said, "Okay, Sara, what else?"

She said, "I learned something else last night, after the

Bible study. I went to a home to baby-sit a little two-year-old boy. Dirtiest kid I have ever seen. When I went into his room, he lifted up his arms to be hugged. I found out, Steve, that it is easier to hug a dirty kid than a stiff kid."

Have you ever had one of those experiences when you understood something for the first time? After Sara left, the Father spoke to me and said, "Child, your dirt is fixable. That is what the Cross is about. It is your stiffness that will kill you. I will hug you when you're dirty, but I will never hug you when you are stiff."

Read Luke 7:36–50. It is one of those dynamite texts in the Bible. It is easier to hug a dirty kid than to hug a stiff kid. When we get into systematizing these principles, it will be important that you remember this one. We are going to face some very hard things about ourselves. That is repentance. And you will see that repentance isn't what you think it is. It is easier to repent when you realize that, when you go to God with all your dirt, He will hug you.

The stiffness is the problem, not the dirt.

God's Love Cannot Be Earned

Now we come to power principle number twelve: *Love in response to goodness is not love—it is reward:*

> The LORD did not set His love on you nor choose you because you were more in number than other people, for you were the least of all peoples. (Deuteronomy 7:7)

> But God demonstrates His own love toward us, in that while we were still sinners, Christ died for us. (Romans 5:8)

I have wonderful daughters. A lot better than yours! But let me tell you something: My daughters are not perfect, and I'm glad that they aren't. Because if they had been perfect, they would never have known that I loved them! It was only when they were not lovable that they knew I loved them.

Why? Because love in response to goodness isn't love—it is reward.

One of the principles I teach the students in seminary is the Protestant equivalent of the Catholic teaching about the priest in his sacramental work: The effectiveness of the sacrament is not dependent upon the purity of the priest. For the Protestant, the principle is this: The effectiveness of the Word is not dependent upon the purity of the preacher.

Allow me to let you in on a preacher's secret: If you want to see a man who is 'fessed up and completely forgiven of all known sin, look at me right before I teach a seminar or preach a sermon. I want you to know that I confess every known sin I have ever committed, and even some that I haven't committed! I do that because preaching and teaching scares me to death, and I don't want to go into any pulpit with any unconfessed sin. I have called people across the country and asked them to forgive me, so that things would be straight between us before I preached.

But let me tell you something else: Sometimes I haven't had time to confess, and have been totally out of fellowship with Christ, angry, judgmental, and bitter. I have gone into the pulpit expecting that God would destroy me. Yet that is when I have preached my most effective sermons! Love in response to goodness is not love, it is reward. You don't earn love. If you earn it, it isn't love. So when the Bible talks about love and grace, it is always in the context of sin and rebellion. The Prodigal Son is not the exception of love, but the very definition of it.

You Can't Love Until You Have Been Loved

Power principle number thirteen: *You can't love until you have been loved.* And even then you can only love to the degree to which you have been loved:

By this we know love, because He laid down His life for us. And we also ought to lay down our lives for the brethren. (1 John 3:16)

A new commandment I give to you, that you love one another; as I have loved you, . . . (John 13:34)

Greater love has no one than this, than to lay down one's life for his friends. You are My friends . . . (John 15:13–14)

People who are free are people who manifest love and forgiveness. You will find freedom in direct proportion to how much you manifest those qualities. Love is the active side of freedom, and forgiveness is its passive side. But you can't just turn the love or forgiveness on. You can only love when you have been loved, and you can only forgive when you have been forgiven.

There was a farm boy by the name of Johnny. He loved Jamie for a long time and never told her. Finally he got up his courage and said, "Jamie, I have been loving you for a long time, and I would be mighty proud if you would be my wife."

She said, "Johnny, I also have been loving you for a long time, and I would be proud to be your wife."

That night Johnny went home and knelt beside his bed, looked up at the stars, and said, "Lord, I ain't got nothin' against nobody now!"

God provided the freedom by forgiving you and by loving you. And you can't get it any other place. So instead of always trying to do things for Him, just be still and let Him love you.

You Can't Forgive Until You Have Been Forgiven

Here's our fourteenth power principle: *You can't forgive*

until you have been forgiven. And you can only forgive to the degree to which you have been forgiven:

> Blessed is he whose transgression is forgiven,
> Whose sin is covered.
> Blessed is the man to whom the LORD does not impute
>   iniquity,
> And in whose spirit there is no deceit. (Psalm 32:1)

A number of years ago, I was discussing with my mother the subject of church discipline. For those of you who are Calvinists, you know that one of the manifestations of a true church is the willingness to practice church discipline. I agree that church discipline is sometimes necessary, but I believe that it should be prescribed, not on the basis of the sin committed, but on the basis of the lack of repentance manifested.

As my mother and I discussed church discipline, she said, "I don't believe that the church ought to be that way."

"But the Bible teaches it," I replied.

She said, "Son, maybe it does teach it . . . but not very much."

Now, my mother was not a Bible scholar and I am. So I thought, *I will look up the hundreds of scriptures on discipline in the Bible. I'll show my mother those hundreds of references, and then she will understand how important it is.* But do you know what? There are *not* hundreds of references to church discipline; in fact, there are very few. The Bible talks about forgiveness and acceptance more than it talks about church discipline.

So I asked myself, *If we talk so much about discipline in the church, and the Bible talks about it far less than we do, what is the problem?* The problem is this: Most people in the church have either never been forgiven or have never felt forgiven. And as a result the church becomes a place of judgment rather than a place of redemption, love, and forgiveness.

Obedience Flows from Freedom

Power principle number fifteen: *Obedience flows from freedom, not freedom from obedience:*

> For I through the law died to the law that I might live to God. (Galatians 2:19)

> I do not set aside the grace of God; for if righteousness comes through the law, then Christ died in vain. (Galatians 2:21)

A lot of people say, "If you teach that stuff, people are going to go and sin, so teach them to be obedient." Well, I have to teach them to be free before they can be obedient. Most of us have it backwards. You see, we think that, if we are obedient enough, and kind enough, and loving enough, then we will be free. That is not true; it works the other way around.

For many years I was sure that God was a policeman. Understanding that He was a *loving* policeman didn't help very much. So, as a recalcitrant child, I worked very hard at pleasing God. I learned to pray regularly (even if it didn't mean anything), to read the Scripture (even if I didn't remember what I read), and, every day in every way, to be a good person—good, kind, loving, gracious, compassionate, involved, and pure.

The problem was that I was *not* a good person, and, no matter how hard I tried, I had to take off the false face every night and look in the mirror. Finally, I was faced (one can act for only so long) with two alternatives: give it up and leave the policeman, accepting whatever punishment was due me; or, go to Him to see if I could be "fixed."

I went to Him, and do you know what happened? He hugged me and told me He had been waiting for me to come. He didn't bring up my sin or my punishment. He just loved me. He told me that my failure was meant to bring me to Him, so that He could love me.

My response to that kind of incredible love has been the only source of growth and obedience in my life. Growth and obedience, for me, has never happened any other way. While I'm still not good . . . I'm better. While I still don't love Him or others as I ought to love . . . I love more than I did. While I haven't manifested all the "fruit of the Spirit" that I ought to manifest . . . you should have seen me before!

Paul put it best:

> For the love of Christ controls us . . . (2 Corinthians 5:14 NASB)

It Was God All Along

One final power principle: *You take the first step; God will take the second step; and by the time you get to the third step, you will know that it was God who took the first step.*

> Work out your own salvation with fear and trembling; for it is God who works in you both to will and to do for His good pleasure. (Philippians 2:12–13)

Some of this stuff we've been learning together may seem too difficult to put into practice. Do it anyway. Sometimes you are not going to want to be honest with yourself. Do it anyway. Sometimes you are not going to want to reach out and be free. Do it anyway. Because the principle is true: If you take the first step, the Father will take the second step, and by the time you get to the third step you will know that it was the Father who took the first step.

8

Seven Steps to Freedom

This issue of our freedom in Christ can be explored from so many different angles. In chapter 5 we explored a process to help you get out of prison, based on the acrostic *R E F L E C T*. In chapter 6 we took a long look at our heavenly Father and learned how His very nature is a liberating thing for us. In chapter 7 we saw that simply understanding how this old fallen world of ours works can be a freeing thing.

Now we're going to take the *seven steps to freedom*. You've probably heard more than you care to hear about "twelve-step" recovery programs. This is the economy size—just seven steps. (I also offer nine commandments and an 8 percent tithe!)

The seven steps we're going to take will be based on the parable of the Prodigal Son. So let's turn to Luke 15 and read together one of the most familiar passages in the Bible:

> A certain man had two sons. And the younger of them said to his father, "Father, give me the portion of goods that falls to me." So he divided to them his livelihood. And not many days after, the younger son gathered all together, journeyed to a far country, and there wasted his possessions with prodigal living. But when he had spent all, there arose a severe famine in that land, and he began to be in want. Then he went and joined himself to a citizen in that country, and he sent him into his fields to feed swine. And he would gladly have filled his stomach with the pods that the swine ate, and no one gave him anything. But when he came to himself, he said, "How many of my father's hired servants have bread enough and to

spare, and I perish with hunger. I will arise and go to my father, and will say to him, 'Father, I have sinned against heaven and before you, and I am no longer worthy to be called your son. Make me like one of your hired servants.'" And he arose and came to his father. But when he was still a great way off, his father saw him and had compassion, and ran and fell on his neck and kissed him. And the son said to him, "Father, I have sinned against heaven and in your sight, and am no longer worthy to be called your son." But the father said to his servants, "Bring out the best robe and put it on him, and put a ring on his hand and sandals on his feet. And bring the fatted calf here and kill it, and let us eat and be merry; for this my son was dead and is alive again; he was lost and is found." And they began to be merry. Now his older son was in the field. And as he came and drew near to the house, he heard music and dancing. So he called one of the servants and asked what these things meant. And he said to him, "Your brother has come, and because he has received him safe and sound, your father has killed the fatted calf." But he was angry and would not go in. Therefore his father came out and pleaded with him. So he answered and said to his father, "Lo, these many years I have been serving you; I never transgressed your commandment at any time; and yet you never gave me a young goat, that I might make merry with my friends. But as soon as this son of yours came, who has devoured your livelihood with harlots, you kill the fatted calf for him." And he said to him, "Son, you are always with me, and all that I have is yours. It was right that we should make merry and be glad, for your brother was dead and is alive again, and was lost and is found." (Luke 15:11–32)

From the story of the Prodigal Son we're going to learn, not just how to leave our prisons, but how to leave our prisons standing up. This is the chapter where we take everything we have learned up to this point and put it into practice.

A farmer's barn was burning down, and he was leaning up against a tree, smoking his corn cob pipe. One of his neighbors said, "Sam, your barn is burning down, do something!"

He said, "I know it's burning; I'm praying for rain."

Christian faith is never quietistic like that. *Quietism,* a heresy taught most notably by Miguel de Molinos, a seventeenth–century Spanish priest, is the belief that all one has to do is be quiet and passive and God will do the rest. Paul was certainly not a quietist. In his letter to the believers at Philippi, he declared,

> I press toward the goal for the prize of the upward call of God in Christ Jesus. (Philippians 3:14)

Christian faith is not passive. If you truly believe that God is sovereign, it is always proper to say, about the past and the present, "Whatever is, is God's will, and I accept it." But it is never proper to say that about the future. Where you are right now, including the fact that you are reading this book, is where you are supposed to be. Every circumstance of your life—every sin, every hurt, every wound, every bit of pain—has been ordained by God. You are where you are supposed to be right now.

But you are not where you are going to be.

What we will learn together over the next few pages is going to enable you to be where you ought to be. As someone has said, "Praise God, I'm not what I was. Praise God, I'm not what I ought to be. But praise God, I'm not what I'm going to be!"

Before we start our journey in the footsteps of the Prodigal Son, let's just catch a glimpse of what we're going to be. Let's sneak a look at the goal of our journey:

> Then the King will say to those on His right hand, "Come, you blessed of My Father, inherit the kingdom prepared for you from the foundation of the world." (Matthew 25:34)

That's our goal, the kingdom God has been getting ready for us since long before we were born. And we can be assured, as Jesus once assured a scribe with a searching heart, that,

> . . . you are not far from the kingdom. (Mark 12:34)

So let's get on with the process. As we consider the story of the Prodigal Son, let's look at how we get from the prison to the palace—from the prisons that enslave, to the glorious freedom God wants us to enjoy. You'll notice that the "seven steps to freedom" we're going to take all begin with the letter *R*. I did that to help you remember them, and to make you think I worked real hard on this!

Realization: Understand *That* It Hurts

The first step on the road from the prison to the palace is *realization*. Acknowledge the fact that you are in prison and that it hurts and that it hurts real bad:

> But when he came to himself . . .

It's an old story, but a good one. A young man came to Socrates and said he wanted to know the truth. Socrates took him down to the river and ducked him under the water and held him there until the young man was struggling for air. He was trying to get up and was sure he was going to drown. When Socrates let him up, he said, "Son, when you want truth in the same way that you just wanted air, then you shall have it."

Remember the principle we learned in chapter 7 about pain—that people are what they have decided to be? When the pain becomes greater than the payback, creative change takes place. I suspect the very fact that you are reading this book is a good indication that the pain in your life has become somewhat acute. When you want relief from your pain as much as that young man wanted air, then you shall have it.

I get letters from all over the country from people who just can't stand the prison anymore. When I was writing *When Being Good Isn't Good Enough*, I asked my radio listeners to write to me about their prisons. In those days only twenty or thirty stations carried my program, but we were simply overwhelmed with stories from all across the country. That's when I started thinking about putting together the seminar this book is based on. I realized that there was a terrible need. People said,

- "I feel guilty all the time."

- "I'm trying to live up to other people's expectations."

- "I don't want to live that way anymore because I can't do it."

- "If God is what they say He is, then I'm in deep trouble."

- "I'm so tired that I can't live this Christian life anymore."

- "I was abused as a child and substituted God for my abuser. I am sure He is going to abuse me as well."

- "If everything is wrong that my pastor says is wrong, the Christian life must be the dullest life in the world."

- "I feel like a failure and I'm tired of feeling that way."

- "I wish I could stand up and tell people what I think, but I always back down."

- "I have this besetting sin and I simply can't get rid of it. What's worse, I don't feel that God has forgiven me, though I have asked Him a thousand times."

- "Do you think that God can ever use me again? I left the church seventeen years ago and I'm afraid to go back."

The list could go on and on. And in every one of those cases and endless others, I could happily say to the person, "You are not very far from the kingdom!"

Why could I say that? Because each of those people were beginning to realize that they were in pain. Did you see the movie *Network*? The leading character in that movie, the news anchorman, goes berserk. They start to take him off the air because it is not a very pretty thing to see a man have a nervous breakdown on camera. But then the ratings start going through the ceiling and they decide to leave him on. On one occasion he asks everyone watching him to open their windows or doors, stick their head out, and yell at the top of their lungs, "I'm mad as hell and I'm not going to take it anymore!" All over the city, hundreds of thousands of people stick their heads out their windows and shout that.

Well, we are Christians, so we can't shout *that*! But I have a vision. It is a vision of hundreds of thousands of Christians all over America shouting in unison, "I'm mad as heaven and I'm not going to take it anymore!"

You say, "Steve, isn't that a little strange?"

No, it isn't. Because heaven *is* mad. God is as mad as you are. Listen to what Paul says in his great treatise on freedom. Now, I want you to understand exactly what Paul is talking about. People had crept into the church and tried to take away the young believers' sense of freedom in Christ. In response, Paul writes,

> But even if we, or an angel from heaven, preach any other gospel to you than what we have preached to you, let him be accursed. (Galatians 1:8)

And later on, he gets even more angry:

> I could wish that those who trouble you would even cut themselves off! (Galatians 5:12)

In other words, "I could wish that they would mutilate themselves."

So you see, one of the things God gets very angry about is when Christians are robbed of their heritage of freedom. We ought to weep when God weeps. We ought to show compassion where God shows compassion. But we also ought to be angry where God shows anger.

Are you tired of feeling guilty all the time?

Are you tired of being manipulated by every religious guru who comes down the pike?

Are you tired of feeling bound by rules?

Are you tired of empty platitudes?

Are you tired of pretending that you are "just fine" when you are not?

Are you tired of pretending to believe stuff you really don't believe?

Are you tired of living in the present with the baggage of your past?

Are you tired of trying to live up to everyone else's expectations?

Are you tired of carrying the load of the whole church on your back?

Are you tired of being responsible for every hurt on the face of the planet?

Are you tired of being afraid all the time?

Do you wish that just for once you could stand up and shout, "Damn!"

Then shout out, "I'm mad as heaven and I'm not going to take it anymore!"

No, I mean really shout it out right now! If you are as mad as heaven—as mad as God is, about the things He is mad about—then you have made the first step away from your prison, toward the palace. Toward the kingdom God has prepared for you.

And that first step is realization.

Recognition: Understand *Why* It Hurts

The second step on our journey from the prison to the palace is *recognition*. Recognition means understanding *why* it hurts:

> But when he came to himself, he said, "How many of my father's hired servants have bread enough and to spare, and I perish with hunger!"

If you are looking for another name for this step, you can call it "denying the denial." Recognition is deeper and more insightful than realization. Realization is knowing that it hurts. Recognition is understanding why it hurts.

You can't always tell everyone the truth, but you must never fail to tell yourself the truth. You can't reveal everything to others, but you must reveal everything to yourself. Most of us are working hard at pretending to be something we aren't. Wouldn't it be nice just to say, "I don't have to pretend anymore"?

Someone tells the story of a man in India who was traveling on a train with all of his earthly possessions. He had them all in a suitcase. He placed the suitcase in the rack above his seat, thinking, *This train is filled with thieves and I have to watch that suitcase very carefully.* So as the hours passed, he watched the suitcase. But along about three o'clock in the morning, he just couldn't keep his eyes open anymore, and for a few seconds he drifted off. When he opened his eyes, the suitcase was gone. He said, "Thank heavens, now I can go to sleep!"

The Bible says, "There is none righteous, no, not one" (Romans 3:10). Are you the exception? You aren't? Good! Now we can be friends. We don't have to pretend anymore. You can go to sleep.

The Bible says the heart is "desperately wicked" (Jeremiah 17:9). Are you the exception? You aren't? Good! Now we can be friends. We don't have to pretend anymore.

The Bible says that everyone has gone his own way (Isaiah 53:6). Are you the exception? No? Good! Now we can be friends. We don't have to pretend anymore.

The Bible says, "Madness is in their hearts while they live, and after that they go to the dead" (Ecclesiastes 9:3). Are you the exception? No? Good! Now we can be friends. We don't have to pretend anymore.

I love this poem by Emily Dickinson:

I'm nobody! Who are you?
Are you nobody, too?
Then there's a pair of us—don't tell!
They'd banish us, you know.

How dreary to be somebody!
How public, like a frog.
To tell your name the livelong day,
 To an admiring bog![12]

Let me give you some statements of denial that are common among Christians:

• "It's really not as bad as it seems."

• At a funeral, people look at the coffin and say, "My, he looks good!" (He doesn't look good, he's dead!)

• Or they say, "I'm basically a good person." (Oh yeah? Ask your wife or husband!)

• Or, "God's will must be done. I must accept every circumstance as from His hand." (That is true. But as the Quaker said to his wife, when she told him not to take his gun because it might be his time to die: "I know, Dear, but thou must remember that it might also be an Indian's time to die.")

• Others in a state of denial will say, "It isn't Christian to be angry."

• Or, "My past is past and those issues don't have any

relevance to my life right now." (Then why do those dogs keep biting you?)

• "Everyone is better than I am," or, "Others know best." (Listen, nobody knows best!)

• "There isn't anything wrong with me, it's the others who need help." (Did you hear about the woman who quit smoking? She was asked if she had become irritable. She said, "No, I have remained my same loving self, but my friends, I have noticed, have become quite unbearable.")

• "I'm a failure because God has ordained me to be a failure. I deserve to fail."

I could go on and on. The point is this: When you are coming out of the prison on the way to the palace, you must look very hard at the reality of the sin and pain in your life, and call it what it is. Of course it is a scary process, but it's not as bad as you think. I have a pastor friend in Chattanooga who dealt with and understood these issues long before I did. I talked with him by phone and told him what I was learning. I said, "I always knew that there were those sleeping dogs in my life, but I was functioning—getting up in the morning and doing what needed to be done. Now that I have time, I'm waking up the dogs.

"However," I told him, "I'm keeping a gun in my hand, and if those dogs try to bite me, I'm going to shoot those suckers."

Sometime later, we were doing a rally in Chattanooga. After the rally, my friend came up to me and said, "Steve, I've got an appointment but I have a message from the Lord for you."

I said, "Well, what is it?"

He said, "The Lord said, 'Go ahead and wake up the dogs; they don't have any teeth.'"

We have one other issue that we need to discuss before moving to the next step. One of the objections I often hear concerning this kind of teaching is that it will cause people to develop a horrible self-image. That is absolute nonsense. Let me tell you how to get a bad self-image: Believe something about yourself that isn't true. You don't get a *good* self-image by saying to yourself, "I'm a wonderful person." You aren't, and that is the worst form of denial.

You say, "I'm really together"? No, you aren't, and that is the worst form of denial.

You say, "I deserve everything I have"? No, you don't, and that is the worst form of denial.

You don't get a good self-image by denying the truth about yourself. A good self-image comes from facing the truth and knowing that, because God accepts you and the whole truth about who you are, you can too.

There is nothing you can ever say to me that will shock me. There is no aberrant behavior you can confess to me that will cause me to think less of you. There is no sin you can confess to me that will cause me to be angry at you. Why? Because there is no sin, no aberrant behavior, and no surprising evil of which I, myself, am not capable.

A number of years ago a friend of mine was going through a horrible depression. He was angry almost all the time. When he was not angry, he was depressed. He was hypercritical of other people. He was hypercritical of himself. One time, on a long shot, I said to him, "Bill, I'm going to set aside three hours on a Saturday morning, and that is the time I'm going to give to you. I'm not going to give you any advice, or tell you what to do, or be your mother. But on Saturday morning, I want you to tell me everything."

"Tell you everything?" he asked.

"Yes, everything."

At first he got angry. He said that there was nothing to tell. He said that he was not going to show up. He told me that I was the one who needed help. But on Saturday morning he was there, and he poured out all of the worst stuff you have ever heard in your life. He started slowly, and then it was like lancing a boil. He talked about his abusive past, his unfaithfulness, a homosexual encounter, a time he had cheated a friend, and all the lies he had told himself and others.

I said, "Bill, there is more. Go on."

Then he told about the times he had thought he was going crazy. Told me about the horrible thoughts he'd had, the irrational behavior he had shown. He told me how he felt about himself, and how dirty he felt sometimes. He told me how he had tried and tried and never quite made it.

Do you know what I said to him? I said, "So what else is new?"

Then he began to cry.

Do you know what I did? I hugged him. Then I told him, "Bill, my reaction to you is the same as God's reaction. I can understand you, and if I can, God can. I love you, and if I can, God can. God told me to tell you that He loves you very much, and He accepts you and you are okay."

That was the day Bill got free. There was such a radical change in his life that it blew everyone away.

He not only felt the pain (*realization*).

He quit denying its source (*recognition*).

Facing his own sin, the reality of his life, his own irresponsibility, he is now free. He went through the pain, to the power.

Responsibility: "I Will Arise and Go"

The third step in our journey is *responsibility*—taking responsibility for your own circumstances and your own pain. Recalling once again the Prodigal Son:

> I will arise and go to my father, and will say to him, "Father, I have sinned against heaven and before you."

Most people who are in prison think it is someone else's

fault that they are there. I once spoke at a women's prison, and afterwards I was standing around talking with some of the women. One of the sweetest, kindest, elderly ladies came up to me. She looked like the universal grandmother. She was soft-spoken, her hair was in a bun. Her eyes twinkled when she spoke. She said, "Mr. Brown, would you pray for me? You know, I'm not guilty of anything, but I am a Christian and have decided to accept my sentence as a call from God to have a ministry in this place. My family—and I love them anyway—my family was the cause of my being here. As the Scripture says, 'they meant it for evil, but God meant it for good.'"

I noticed that a friend of mine, a former prisoner himself who now had a wonderful prison ministry, was standing over in the corner laughing. After the lady left, I asked him why he was laughing. "Steve," he said, "do you know what that woman did to get in here?"

I allowed that I didn't, but I was sure it wasn't all that bad.

He said, "She owned a nursing home. She doused one of her elderly residents with gasoline and set her on fire!"

Most people in prison think it is someone else's fault they are there. In the *Book of Worship of the Church of Scotland*, one of the prayers of confession includes this phrase: "I have sinned in my own fault." "Owning up" is one of the most important steps on the road to freedom. We have learned, over the preceding chapters, that our past can affect us in the present, and that we live in a fallen world; that knowledge should lead us to deeper understanding, not to better excuses.

When I began discovering the issues of my own past, at first I felt relief that I was no longer responsible for my behavior. When I learned about my grandfather's suicide; when I began dealing with the fact that my father had had a mistress; when I realized my fear of abandonment . . . I said, "That's great! I'm not responsible for all the bad stuff I've done."

And then I stopped growing.

That was when a friend told me what I am telling you: Understanding is not another word for excuse.

Take responsibility.

Repentance: Agree with God

The fourth step toward the palace of freedom is *repentance*. Repentance simply means agreeing with God about what needs to be changed in your life:

> I will arise and go to my father, and will say to him, "Father, I have sinned against heaven and before you, and I am no longer worthy to be called your son. Make me like one of your hired servants."

Of all the steps on the road to the palace, this is the most important.

Let me ask you something: If your sin has been forgiven—past, present, and future; if you never have to feel guilty again; if God has covered you, and as Corrie ten Boom says, has dumped the sin in the ocean and put up a sign that says "no fishing"; if all that is true, why should you confess your sins before God?

As we have noted, there are those who say, "When you become a Christian, God gives you a clean slate," but that is a lie. God doesn't give you a clean slate; He tears up the slate and throws it away and never gives you another one to replace it. He doesn't keep track anymore, because He is no longer a scorekeeper or a policeman or a judge—He is your Father.

So if all of that is true, why confess? Because the life of power, freedom, and wholeness is a life of repentance; and confession is an important part of repentance.

Now, before we go any further, it is important that we define repentance. Repentance is a wonderful biblical word, and we have allowed the neurotic Christians and the angry pagans to define it for us. That is a great tragedy. In the Old Testament, the word *repentance* comes from a word meaning "to comfort." How about that! In the New Testament it means to change one's mind. It has nothing to do with the weirdo who walks down the street saying, "Repent! The end is near!" Repentance means nothing more nor less than agreeing with God about who you are, what you have done, and what needs to be changed.

Implicit in that agreement with God is a feeling of total helplessness. Jack Miller, who teaches much of what I'm teaching, says that the pastor of the church ought to be the most repentant person in the congregation. Why is that? Because he is the leader, and that is the point of leadership— the leader is the person who agrees with God the most!

Repentance does not mean changing, or becoming a super-Christian, or engaging in self-flagellation. Repentance is simply agreeing with God about who you are, what you have done, and what you need to change. I used to think that repentance couldn't be repentance unless there was true change. If that is true, most of us have never repented. In the case of the son in Jesus' story, repentance involved going to the Father. That is what repentance is. It is going to the Father. Repentance is saying, with Paul,

> The good that I will to do, I do not do; but the evil I will not to do that I practice. . . . O wretched man that I am! Who will deliver me from this body of death? (Romans 7:19, 24)

It is saying, with Paul, "I am the chief of sinners" (1 Timothy 1:15).

Job 38:2–3 is the key passage in that whole book. It is nothing more nor less than a call for Job's repentance:

> Who is this who darkens counsel
> By words without knowledge?
> Now prepare yourself like a man;

I will question you, and you shall answer Me.

And Job's response to God is nothing more nor less than his repentance:

Then Job answered the LORD and said:

"I know that You can do everything,
And that no purpose of Yours can be withheld from You.
You asked, 'Who is this who hides counsel without
  knowledge?'
Therefore I have uttered what I did not understand,
Things too wonderful for me, which I did not know.
Listen, please, and let me speak;
You said, 'I will question you, and you shall answer Me.'

"I have heard of You by the hearing of the ear,
But now my eyes see You.
Therefore I abhor myself,
And repent in dust and ashes." (Job 42:1–6)

Repentance is going to God, allowing Him to be God, and accepting His loving judgment. Remember, Job's humble repentance led to his full restoration.

A number of years ago a particular denomination issued a report on human sexuality. Among other things, it suggested that we should no longer label as sin such things as fornication, homosexuality, adultery, or pornography. When I heard of the report I was so angry that I literally could not speak. I stood in the pulpit holding the report on human sexuality in my hand and was so angry that I couldn't even speak. I apologized to the congregation, sat down, and tried to compose myself.

Never before had I experienced anger that made me speechless. Usually, the angrier I become, the better I talk. After praying about it, I realized that for one of the few times in my life, I was experiencing the anger of God—and it was a fearsome thing to behold!

Listen carefully: God was not angry because of the sin of

homosexuality, fornication, adultery, or pornography. Does that surprise you? God was angry—and I believe that I expressed that anger in my speechlessness—because the report had said that sin was not sin, thus burning the bridge of repentance, which is the only real source of power for the Christian. The report's horror was not that it seemed to forgive some horrible sin. God does that all the time. The report's horror was that it said that there was no need for forgiveness.

Do you have a "besetting sin?" I have a number of them. But the real problem with those sins is not that God hasn't forgiven them. The problem is that we become so embarrassed that we don't go to God in repentance anymore. We say, "I have confessed this sin and this behavior to God so many times, that He must be getting tired of it. I haven't changed and I don't see any prospect for change. I just can't confess it anymore. God will know that I'm insincere." And we turn away from God.

I am convinced that this is the reason so many people have left the faith. They just couldn't measure up, and so they just quit trying.

Of course you don't measure up! But don't ever stop going to God with a heart of repentance. Without that there is nothing. Repentance—agreeing with God—is the key to everything. It prevents you from being judgmental of others; it opens the gate of power to escape from your prison; and it is the method whereby—however slowly it happens—we change.

Remorse: Allow Yourself to Grieve

The fifth step on the way from the prison to the palace—after realization, recognition, responsibility, and repentance—is *remorse*. That means allowing yourself to feel grief as you say goodbye to your old self. It means being willing to go through the Crucifixion before getting to the Resurrection. We don't see this step specifically in the story of the Prodigal Son, but we do see remorse displayed a number of other places in the Bible:

> Therefore I abhor myself,
> And repent in dust and ashes. (Job 42:6)

> "Now, therefore," says the LORD,
> "Turn to Me with all your heart,
> With fasting, with weeping, and with mourning."
> So rend your heart, and not your garments;
> Return to the LORD your God,
> For He is gracious and merciful,
> Slow to anger, and of great kindness. (Joel 2:12)

When Oswald Chambers decided to make a total commitment of his life to God, he went through great pain. He wrote a poem on that occasion which included these lines:

> . . . Never can I live in gladness,
> Never can I turn from sadness,
>   But I must dwell in tears.

You have probably heard of the five steps to the grieving process: (1) shock, (2) anger, (3) depression, (4) bargaining, and (5) acceptance. When a person starts moving out of prison, toward freedom, he or she goes through exactly the same process. The prison may not be nice, but it is all we have known. It is far easier to keep saying to yourself that you are a nice person, than to face the truth. Freedom is, at least at first, a place of high anxiety and very little security. Prison, on the other hand, can be warm and comfortable. It is difficult at first to admit that the thing which gave you so much comfort is really a dank, musty old prison. Making such an admission involves remorse and mourning.

My friend Larry Crabb, in his book *Inside Out*, talks about how we must go through the pain before getting to the healing. The pain is the surgeon's knife and it is important.

We must go through the Crucifixion before getting to the Resurrection. So let's go through the grieving process together, as we think about breaking out of our prisons. Let's imagine what kind of thoughts might be going through our minds as we leave our prisons and go through each of the five stages of grieving:

1. Shock: "I'm not the person I thought I was." . . . "There's so much bad stuff in me." . . . "I'm so ashamed." . . . "My parents weren't as good as I thought they were." . . . "My pastor isn't perfect." . . . "My hero isn't my hero anymore." . . . "I can't believe I'm really like this." . . . "Man, this really hurts." . . .

2. Anger: "How could they do that to me?" . . . "They betrayed me." . . . "How could God let this happen to me?" . . . "I'm tired of this guilt trip." . . . "I'm not that bad and I won't allow others to think that of me." . . .

3. Depression: "I'll never be different." . . . "I've been this way all my life and there's no hope for me." . . . "How could I be so stupid, so sinful, and so ignorant?" . . . "I'll just spend my life in tears." . . .

4. Bargaining: "Lord, if You will allow me to just keep a bit myself, I'll be good." . . . "I'll just wait and my ship will come in, won't it, Lord?" . . . "I did something bad today, but I'll do something good tomorrow, and that will balance things out . . . won't it?" . . .

5. Acceptance: "Father, I'm not much, but I'm Yours." . . . "If I were You, I wouldn't spend much time on me, but for whatever reason You have loved me and forgiven me." . . . "You promised that even if I never get any better, You will still love me and accept me. If You can do that, I guess I can too." . . .

Someone sent me a wonderful story from a book titled, *Mortal Lessons: Notes on the Art Of Surgery*, by Richard Selzer, a professor at Yale Medical School:

I stand by the bed where a young woman lies, her face post-operative, her mouth twisted in palsy, clownish. A tiny twig of the facial nerve, the one to the muscles of her mouth, has been severed. She will be thus from now on. The surgeon had followed with religious fervor the curve of her flesh; I promise you that. Nevertheless, to remove the tumor in her cheek, I had to cut the little nerve.

Her young husband is in the room. He stands on the opposite side of the bed, and together they seem to dwell in the evening lamplight, isolated from me, private. Who are they, I ask myself, he and this wry mouth I have made, who gaze at each other and touch each other so generously, greedily? The young woman speaks.

"Will my mouth always be like this?" she asks.

"Yes," I say, "it will. It is because the nerve was cut."

She nods and is silent. But the young man smiles.

"I like it," he says. "It is kind of cute."

All at once I know who he is. I understand, and I lower my gaze. One is not bold in an encounter with a god. Unmindful, he bends to kiss her crooked mouth, and I so close I can see how he twists his own lips to accommodate hers, to show that their kiss still works.[13]

Do you see it? That is what the God of the universe has done in Christ. He has twisted His mouth to make sure the kiss still works. He has grieved over your sin far more than you ever will. Yet He accepts you just the same. He enables you to take that fifth and final step of acceptance.

John Bradshaw has a wonderful way of helping the people in his seminars say goodbye to their parents, that is, to deal once and for all with the prisons their parents had put them in. He asks people to imagine taking themselves, as a little boy or girl, back to view all of the events of the past. Then they take their lost child by the hand and leave, waving goodbye to the parents.

Try this: Close your eyes and imagine a letter you would write to your parents. Then open your eyes and write it . . . but don't ever send it. Write a letter to your old self; write a letter to those who have made you feel guilty; just don't ever send the letters.

Then burn the letters. Cry, weep, and mourn, but burn them. It is the beginning of your freedom.

Relinquishment: "I Can't Help Myself"

There is realization, recognition, responsibility, repentance, remorse, and then the sixth step from the prison to the palace is *relinquishment*. Admit that you still lack power over the prison.

> I am no longer worthy to be called your son. Make me like one of your hired servants.

Step one of the twelve-step programs is to admit that you are powerless over the problem. That principle is important for anyone who would be free from a prison.

Now, you may see an apparent contradiction here. I have said that you are not helpless, that you don't have to stay the same way, and now I'm saying that you are helpless. The contradiction is only apparent. The way you become *not* helpless, is to *be* helpless. As we have already noted, the American folk religion says, "God helps those who help themselves," but the Bible says, "God helps those who can't help themselves and know it."

Let me give you a "power psalm," and explain how God used it in the life of John Wesley. Wesley was an English Anglican priest. He was the leader of the "Holy Club" at Oxford. He was a missionary, and a scholar . . . and a failure. On going to America as a missionary, he wrote in his diary, "I'm going to Georgia to save the heathen, but, Oh God, who will save me?" Of course if you had known Wesley at the time, you would not have guessed that such a struggle was going on inside. You probably would have said, "How strong, how secure, how spiritual he is."

Wesley made all kinds of promises to God. He promised to be more faithful, to pray more and work harder. Then it all fell apart on him. He failed as a missionary. He had "woman troubles." He fled his post. He blew the whole thing. On the evening of May 22, 1738, he was in his room and his Bible fell open to the 130th Psalm:

> Out of the depths I have cried to You, O LORD;
> Lord, hear my voice!
> Let Your ears be attentive
> To the voice of my supplications.
>
> If You, O LORD, should mark iniquities,
> O Lord, who could stand?
> But there is forgiveness with You,
> That You may be feared.
>
> I wait for the LORD, my soul waits,
> And in His word I do hope.
> My soul waits for the Lord
> More than those who watch for the morning—
> Yes, more than those who watch for the morning.
>
> O Israel, hope for the LORD;
> For with the LORD there is mercy,
> And with Him is abundant redemption.
> And He shall redeem Israel
> From all his iniquities.

The next day, May 24th, Wesley went to a small meeting of Christians at Aldersgate, where he heard Martin Luther's preface to his commentary on the Book of Romans being read. For the first time he understood that God helps those who can't help themselves and know it. He wrote in his diary, "My heart was strangely warmed." That was the beginning of one of the greatest spiritual awakenings the world has ever seen. And much of American Christianity exists today because John Wesley found that he was really helpless. Relinquishment is a necessary step on the way from the prison to the palace.

Relinquishment means letting go of the need to control. Catherine Marshall had gone to Washington to serve with her husband, Peter Marshall, at a nationally famous Presbyterian church. Shortly after arriving there, she contracted a disease that confined her to her bed. She wanted to help her husband. She had so much to do. But she didn't get any better. She decided that her sickness was the result of her sin, but still she stayed sick. She wrote to everyone she had ever hurt or offended. She even wrote to an elementary school where she had cheated on an exam in second grade. But she stayed sick.

Finally, after weeks of frustration, Catherine said, "God, I hate this. I'm no help to You or to anyone else on this bed, but if this is the way You want me to be for the rest of my life, I relinquish it to You." From that moment on, she began to get better.

Prisoners who think that they can get out of the prison by themselves, stay there forever. Almost every one of those prisons we explored back in chapter 1 results from wanting to be in control. Relinquishment of that control is a necessary step for the Christian who wants to be free.

That reminds me again of the sage observation of my friend Israel Moses Kreps: "I have learned that there is only one messiah per universe, and I'm not it."

Another friend of mine said, "Worry and guilt are both manifestations of the same phenomenon—*fear*. Worry is fear looking forward, and guilt is fear looking backward." Relinquishment means freedom from fear. Paul wrote to Timothy in 2 Timothy 1:7:

> For God has not given us a spirit of fear, but of power and of love and of a sound mind.

You can trust God to run His universe. You can trust God to run your family. You can trust God to be the God of your life. He won't fail you, ever.

As long as you *don't* want Him to have control, however, He will let you stay in charge. And your control will build more bars in the prison door.

Resolution: Accept Your Freedom

The seventh and final step from the prison to the palace is *resolution*. Accept the fact that the price has been paid for your freedom:

> But the father said to his servants, "Bring out the best robe and put it on him, and put a ring on his hand and sandals on his feet. And bring the fatted calf here and kill it, and let us eat and be merry; for this my son was dead and is alive again; he was lost and is found." And they began to be merry.

Paul Harvey tells of the time when Dr. A. J. Gordon, the famous Boston minister, came into his pulpit with a bird cage. Once he had everyone's attention, Dr. Gordon said that, just the day before, he had met a boy who was carrying that bird cage, and the cage was filled with birds.

"Where did you get those birds, son?" he had asked the boy.

"I caught them," the boy replied.

"What are going to do with them?" Dr. Gordon asked.

"I'm going to play with them."

"Well," the pastor said, "you can't play with them forever. What are you going to do with them when you are finished playing with them?"

"Well, sir," the boy said, "I have some cats, and when I'm finished playing with them, I'll give them to the cats."

"Son," Dr. Gordon said, "What would you take for those birds?"

"You don't want these birds, sir. They're just field birds. They're not worth nothin'."

Dr. Gordon repeated his offer: "What would you take for them?"

The boy thought about it. "Well, you can have them for two dollars."

The transaction was made. The boy walked away with the two dollars and Dr. Gordon walked away with the birds.

He walked into an alley between two buildings and let the birds go free.

Then Dr. Gordon told another story:

Once Satan met God in the Garden of Eden. Satan had a cage. "What do you have in that cage?" God asked.

"Some humans," Satan replied.

"Where did you get them?"

"I caught them."

"What are you going to do with them?"

"Well," Satan said, "I'm going to play with them."

"You can't play with them forever. What are you going to do with them when you are finished playing with them?"

Satan said, "I'm going to kill them and then damn them."

"What would you take for them?" God asked.

"You don't want these humans," Satan said. "They will just spit on You and curse You and turn away from You."

"How much?"

"Well," Satan said, "If You want to know how much I would take, it would take all of Your tears and all of Your blood. . . ."

The transaction was made. God paid the price, got the cage, opened the door, and let all the humans go free.

You are free. God has paid the price, and you don't have to pay it anymore.

Realize that the cage is a cage.

Recognize why you are there.

Take *responsibility* for your being there.

Repent, by agreeing with God's assessment of the cage.

Let yourself go through the grieving of *remorse*.

Relinquish control over the cage.

Then, as you take the final step of *resolution*, accepting the freedom God offers through Jesus Christ, He will open the cage and you will fly out, free as a bird.

You think about that.

Afterword: Your Freedom in Action

Now I want to talk to those of you who have come to an understanding of radical grace, who have studied the Bible deeply enough to understand God's total acceptance of you and forgiveness of you no matter what. If you understand radical grace and radical freedom, there is a major danger. Satan will always find a way to use 99 percent of the truth to float one lie. The lie that often creeps into teachings on radical grace and freedom is that you can use the freedom to justify self-centeredness. This is what Paul was concerned about when he wrote to the Galatians:

> For you, brethren, have been called to liberty; only do not use liberty as an opportunity of the flesh, but through love serve one another. (Galatians 5:13)

Paul seems to be saying that true freedom involves servanthood. Perhaps that is the key to avoiding the pitfall of self-centeredness. Let's take a look at how, for the Christian, freedom and servanthood go together.

Then we'll see how, as free men and women, we can serve our brothers and sisters in Christ by introducing them to the freedom we have found.

After we've done that, we'll consider how people who know Christ's perfect freedom should relate to those who do not know Christ at all.

In a word, let's explore some ways to put our freedom in action.

Free as a Slave!

In Exodus 21 Moses gives Israel some laws concerning slaves. Slavery was allowed in the Old Testament, but there was an interesting hitch. When a Hebrew slave had served six years, he or she was allowed to go free. But the Law also addressed the question of what to do if the slave did not *want* to go free:

> But if the servant plainly says, "I love my master, my wife, and my children; I will not go out free," then his master shall bring him to the judges. He shall also bring him to the door, or to the doorpost, and his master shall pierce his ear with an awl; and he shall serve him forever. (Exodus 21:5–6)

A person who chose to remain a servant for life, without at all being coerced to do so, was called a bondservant. And that is what a Christian is. Romans 1:1: "Paul, a bondservant of Jesus Christ . . ."

Let me use the symbolism of the bondservant's pierced ear to help you see why being Christ's bondservant is an important ingredient in our freedom as Christians.

First, the pierced ear of the bondservant is *freely chosen*:

> Jesus answered them, "Most assuredly, I say to you, whoever commits sin is a slave of sin. And a slave does not abide in the house forever, but a son abides forever. Therefore if the Son makes you free, you shall be free indeed." (John 8:34–36)

One of the problems with most teaching on freedom is that there's always a kicker. That's how the cults get people involved. Back in the sixties I watched the Children of God work their scam. They would bring a bunch of young people on a bus to a place where there were throngs of young people congregating. The kids from the Children of God would begin to mix. The other kids would see their laughter, their obvious joy, and their freedom. The bus would load up again, but the number in the bus would be higher because a lot of other kids had joined the Children of God. Later those kids would find out about the sleepless nights, the unbelievable rules, the subtle manipulation, and the requirement that they completely separate themselves from "the world"—including their parents, their church, and their friends. If there is ever a kicker on someone's teaching on freedom, then it is no longer freedom.

A friend of mine told me he had started going to a church because the church was so free. I saw him several months later and he had stopped attending that church. I asked him why, and he said it was all a sham. They were just like everybody else. After they got you in they told you about the rules.

As we have seen, freedom doesn't come from obedience, obedience comes from freedom. If we ever get that backwards, we have destroyed what Jesus went through a lot of trouble establishing.

During the Second World War, a nurse was doing the kind of hard stuff nurses do and a reporter said to her, "Sister, I wouldn't do that for a million dollars."

And she replied, "Brother, I wouldn't do this for a million dollars either."

In other words, she was saying, "I'm not a conscript. I'm a volunteer."

If you are never obedient, will God still love you? Yes, He will. If you never reach out to your brothers and sisters in Christ to help them be free, will God still accept you? Yes, He will. If your witness in the world is lousy, will God still give you eternal life? Yes! A thousand times yes!

We are volunteer bondservants. We have asked the master to pierce our ears and claim us forever as His own.

Second, the pierced ear is *supremely normal*:

> For if we are beside ourselves, it is for God; or if we are of
> sound mind, it is for you. For the love of Christ compels us,
> because we judge thus: that if One died for all, then all died;
> and He died for all, that those who live should live no longer
> for themselves, but for Him who died for them and rose
> again. (2 Corinthians 5:13–15)

We've always had German shepherds. The first was
Barnabas, who is now in doggie heaven. I discussed
philosophy with him. The second was Calvin, the Dumb
One, whose intelligence was the equivalent of an amoeba.
The third was Gandalf, who died before the age of
accountability. We are now on our fourth one and his name is
Quincy the Wonder Dog.

But let me tell you about Calvin.

Calvin was the dumbest dog we've ever had. In fact, he
was the dumbest dog I've ever known. He liked to play with
the ball, and when I would take the ball and hold it behind
my back, he would look at me and say, "You're so smart! You
made that ball disappear!" Annie Dillard, in her Pulitzer
Prize winning *Pilgrim at Tinker Creek*, talks about the
difference in the eyes of farm animals and wild animals. She
says farm animals have eyes that are vacant and dead, while
wild animals have eyes that are alive and free. Well, Calvin's
eyes looked sort of like the eyes of a cow.

Calvin was our orphan. He just showed up at our house
one night. He had mange, and the filthiest white coat you
have ever seen, with cuts and scrapes all over his body.
When we took him to the vet, he said that the dog had
obviously been mercilessly beaten and then discarded on the
roadside. Calvin was the dumbest dog we ever had, but he
was also the most loving and loyal dog we ever had. You see,
he had been beaten and now he was loved. He had been
hungry and now he was fed. He had been hated and now he
was loved.

His loyalty and love came from serving a new master.

Someone told me about an ad in a newspaper that read, "Lost dog. Suffers from mange, missing one eye, walks with a limp. Answers to the name Lucky." You know that dog was lucky—because he was loved! So was Calvin. In the words of the apostle Peter,

> But you are a chosen generation, a royal priesthood, a holy nation, His own special people, that you may proclaim the praises of Him who called you out of darkness into His marvelous light; who once were not a people but are now the people of God, who had not obtained mercy but now have obtained mercy. (1 Peter 2:9–10)

If all that is true, it is no wonder that Peter would write, a few verses later,

> For you were like sheep going astray, but have now returned to the Shepherd and the Overseer of your souls (2:25)

You've never seen a man who wants to please God more than I do. Why? So He'll love me? No, He already loves me. So He'll forgive me? No, He's already forgiven me. So He'll give me eternal life? No, He's already given me eternal life. Listen, and I'm going to give you a life-changing principle: Almost all progress in obedience comes—not from committing yourself to making progress in obedience—but from responding to the One who will love you even if you never ever make any progress in obedience.

You say, "Steve, will you repeat that?"

Yes, I will: Almost all progress in obedience comes, not from committing yourself to making progress in obedience, but from responding to the One who will love you even if you never ever make any progress in obedience.

Third, the pierced ear is *clearly appropriate*: Isaiah 6 is one of my favorite chapters in the entire Bible. It was the year

King Uzziah died and Isaiah, who was an official in the temple, was polishing a golden candleholder and whistling a Jewish hymn when God paid him a visit. God was not what Isaiah had expected. In fact, anyone who has ever met the real God of the universe will never be flippant when he or she meets that God for the second time.

Isaiah saw an amazing vision of God, complete with angels and smoke and fire. The angels cried out,

> Holy, holy, holy is the LORD of hosts;
> The whole earth is full of His glory! (Isaiah 6:3)

Then in verse 5, Isaiah responded,

> Woe is me, for I am undone!
> Because I am a man of unclean lips,
> And I dwell in the midst of a people of unclean lips;
> For my eyes have seen the King,
> The LORD of hosts.

Dear friend, that is the appropriate response of a Christian who has encountered the real God. It isn't a warm, fuzzy feeling; it is awesome fear. If you have never stood before God and been afraid, you have never stood before God. Let me say it again: If you have never stood before God and been afraid, you have never stood before the real God.

Did you hear about the archbishop who went to the cathedral for his evening prayers, knelt down before the high altar, and prayed "OOhh, God," and a voice said, "Yes, what is it?" The next morning they found the archbishop in the cathedral, dead of a coronary. Just as Lewis's Aslan is not a tame lion, our God is not a God to be trifled with.

I once visited the White House, in the company of Bill Lukash, who was President Nixon's physician. Those were the days when Nixon attended the church where I was pastor. Bill took me around the White House, behind the scenes, and I was—you would have been proud of me—quite cool. He showed me the secret service headquarters and I said, "That's nice." He showed me the Oval Office and I was overwhelmed on the inside but said only, "That's nice," because I was so cool.

Finally, Bill took me to his own office. He pushed the phone over to me and said, "Steve, you can call any place in the world on that phone. Just pick it up and the White House operator will instantly put you in touch with anyone you want to talk to—anywhere. Want to try?"

And I said, "No, Bill, but it is interesting."

But he insisted, so I called Anna. And that's when I lost it. I said, "Anna, you're not gonna believe where I'm calling you from!"

That day I learned why a man could sell his soul in the White House. You think to yourself, *This is the seat of the most awesome power in the universe. From here decisions are made that change the course of history. This is the place where history resides.*

I realized that, if I were to get a job in the White House, I would probably do anything to hold onto the power it represents.

Is that an appropriate response in the face of human power? Of course not. However, such a response is altogether appropriate when the power you are responding to is God's power. Once I have encountered God, my normal and appropriate impulse is to fall on my knees.

Someone tells the story of a man who met King George of England at a reception. In casual conversation the king said to the man, "It would be nice for you to come to lunch sometime."

The next day the man turned up at the castle at noon. The guard informed the king, and the king came down to the man and said, "I'm glad you came, but it was just a suggestion. You didn't have to come today."

The man replied, "Your majesty, the king's suggestions are my commands."

Fourth, the pierced ear is *obviously prudent*:

Oh, how I love Your law!
It is my meditation all the day.
You, through Your commandments,
  make me wiser than my enemies. (Psalm 119:97–98)

The Jews consider Holy Torah God's greatest gift to them, because it teaches them how to live. It is their guide to how the universe works. If I were not a Christian, I'd still try to live by the Law of God. You know why? Because my mother didn't have a dumb child!

In chapter 6, I mentioned Max Weber's concept of the "Protestant work ethic." The term is often used with derision by twitty economics professors who, if they didn't receive a salary for saying such stupid things, would be among the homeless. Let me tell you something: The Protestant work ethic produced the greatest national wealth the world has ever seen. George Gilder, in his very good book, *Wealth and Poverty*,[14] says that democracy won't work without faith, and faith produces wealth. In other words, being obedient to God is not only proper, it is very wise and prudent. God didn't say not to commit adultery because He's against your having a good time; He told you not to do it because it exacts a horrible price. Same thing with murder and Sabbath-breaking and stealing and bearing false witness and coveting. You see, I've done it my way and I've done it His way: And, dear friend, His way is best.

Fifth, the pierced ear is *supernaturally motivated*: Our willingness to serve comes, not from our own goodness, but from Christ's indwelling presence:

For I through the law died to the law that I might live to God.
I have been crucified with Christ; it is no longer I who live,
but Christ lives in me; and the life which I now live in the

flesh I live by faith in the Son of God, who loved me and gave Himself for me. (Galatians 2:19–20)

One Sunday a number of years ago, when I was a pastor and when we didn't know what caused AIDS but we knew that it was a killer and suspected you could get it just by looking at someone funny, I was walking quickly from the pulpit to my study at the church. I've always hated the ritual of standing at the door of the church and, since I didn't have to do it in the early service, my object was always to get from the pulpit to my study before anyone could stop me.

Well, this time I was stopped by a young man who grabbed me by the arm and said, "Mr. Brown, could I talk to you?"

I said, "Well, son, you can talk to me if you can talk fast and walk with me."

Then the young man stopped and held my arm. Looking into my eyes he said, "Mr. Brown, I have AIDS, and I'm dying."

You know what I did? I hugged him. I held him while he cried.

Then, when I got back to my study and I realized what I had done, I thought to myself, *I don't believe I did that!*

And God said, "You didn't, I did."

There are too many phony Christians around, playing like they're Christians. Listen: Considering our sinful tendencies, the fallenness of the world, and the attractiveness of sin, obedience is a supernatural work. It is one of those things that, in the words of Ian Thomas, can only be explained in terms of the supernatural. Frank Sinatra sings, "I did it my way." His way was not the best way. But, because you are a Christian and God's Spirit is in you, you can do it *your* way with far better results. That's why Augustine could say, "Love God, and do as you please." You see, obedience is a supernatural thing that happens inside. It all comes from God's Spirit.

Finally, the pierced ear is *deliriously joyful*:

> These things I have spoken to you, that My joy may remain in you, and that your joy may be full. (John 15:11)

When I was installed as pastor of a church near Boston, I asked one of my professors at Boston University to preach the installation sermon. It wasn't that I thought he would say anything biblical. I didn't *know* anything biblical at that time and neither did he. However he did tell good jokes, and installation services are notoriously dull, and if his jokes were good the evening wouldn't be a total loss.

Shortly after he was into the sermon he told a joke that I had heard him tell on numerous occasions with everybody laughing. In my church, nobody laughed. In fact, on numerous occasions in the sermon he said some very funny things and nobody laughed. After the service we were in my study and his only comment was, "Son, you are now the pastor of a very staid church."

It was at that church that I began to learn some important things about the truth of the Bible and the nature of the Christian walk. And being a teacher, I taught the congregation what I was learning. That church, dear friend, exploded. Many, many people were saved. A missions program was begun. The budget doubled. The church was full of college students. And all of those things were good. But the best thing that happened was that those dear people learned to laugh.

There is a direct correlation between one's proximity to Christ and the freedom of one's laughter. Let me repeat it: There is a direct correlation between one's proximity to Christ and the freedom of one's laughter. Christians laugh easily because they don't have to be God anymore. Christians laugh easily because they have a secret. Christians laugh easily because in His service there is great joy.

One of the great tragedies of modern literature is that evil is portrayed as exciting and fun, while good is portrayed as bland and mournful. Dear friend, that is a lie from the pit of hell and it smells like smoke. I once performed a wedding at a circus, between a fire-eater and a grounds keeper. It was an interesting occasion. There was a transvestite in the circus choir who wanted to know the color of the bride's dress so his would match. There was a recessional on an elephant. I did the ceremony in the center ring of the circus, between shows.

During that wedding I got to see what it was really like behind the scenes at a circus. I had always wanted to run away with the circus. Not any more. I've seen the truth. The beautiful ladies are just tired, not beautiful. The handsome men are ugly on ugly. There is no fun—it's all an up-front show. Obedience is the real source of joy, and knowing the pleasure of God is the real place of laughter.

In John Bunyan's *Pilgrim's Progress*, Christiana hears Mercy laugh in her sleep and the next morning asks her why she had laughed. Mercy says that she had had a dream, and in the dream she was dirty, dressed in rags, bemoaning her hardness of heart. Then an angel came to her and asked her what was wrong and she told him.

Mercy then describes what happened next:

Now when he had heard me make my complaint, he said, Peace be to thee. He also wiped mine eyes with his Handkerchief, and clad me in Silver and Gold: he put a Chain about my Neck, and Earrings in mine Ears, and a beautiful Crown upon my Head. Then he took me by the Hand, and said, Mercy, come after me. So he went up, and I followed, till we came at a Golden Gate. Then he knocked; and when they within had opened, the man went in, and I followed him up to a Throne, upon which one sat, and he said to me, Welcome, Daughter. The place looked bright and twinkling like the Stars, or rather like the Sun, and I thought that I saw your Husband there. So I awoke from my Dream. But did I laugh?[15]

The free Christian isn't always obedient. But when he or she is, laughter—free laughter that can come from no place else—comes from the throne and is reflected in the believer. It is called joy, and you can't get it from anywhere else.

Freedom for Others

One of the most joyful services we can perform as free men and women is to share our new-found freedom with our brothers and sisters in Christ:

> So He came to Nazareth, where He had been brought up. And as His custom was, He went into the synagogue on the Sabbath day, and stood up to read. And He was handed the book of the prophet Isaiah. And when He had opened the book, He found the place where it was written:
>
> > The Spirit of the LORD is upon Me,
> > Because He has anointed Me to preach the gospel to the poor;
> > He has sent Me to heal the brokenhearted,
> > To proclaim liberty to the captives
> > And recovery of sight to the blind,
> > To set at liberty those who are oppressed:
> > To proclaim the acceptable year of the LORD.
>
> Then He closed the book and gave it back to the attendant and sat down. And the eyes of all who were in the synagogue were fixed on Him. And He began to say to them, "Today this Scripture is fulfilled in your hearing." (Luke 4:16–21)
>
> So Jesus said to them again, "Peace to you! As the Father has sent Me, I also send you." And when He had said this, He breathed on them, and said to them, "Receive the Holy Spirit. If you forgive the sins of any, they are forgiven them; if you retain the sins of any, they are retained." (John 20:21–23)

Archimandrite Sophrony was a famous Russian artist who after the Russian Revolution studied at the Orthodox Theological Institute in Paris. He eventually went to Mount

Athos, a monastic retreat of Orthodox Christendom where he spent twenty-two years. Then for the last seven years of his life he was a hermit in the desert. In his book *His Life Is Mine*, Sophrony writes,

> The first sign of emancipation is a disinclination to impose one's will on others. The second—an inner release from the hold of others on oneself. Mastery over the wish to dominate is an extremely important stage which is closely followed by dislike of constraining our brother. Man is made in the image of God, Who is humble but at the same time free. Therefore it is normal and natural that he should be after the likeness of his Creator—that he should recoil from exercising control over others while himself being free and independent by virtue of the presence of the Holy Spirit within him. Those who are possessed by the lust for power cloud the image of God in themselves. The light of true life departs, leaving a tormenting void, a distressing tedium. Life is bereft of meaning. When the Holy Spirit by its gentle presence in our soul enables us to master our passions we realize that to look down on others is contrary to the spirit of love.[16]

I see you becoming part of an army of Christians who will revolutionize the church. Why is that? Because free people have a responsibility to help others become free. A missionary tells the story of a blind man who, after cataract surgery in a mission hospital, had his sight restored. Three days later he came back to the hospital pulling a rope. Twenty-three blind people were holding on to the rope! He had brought them to the hospital to receive their sight!

Guilty people make others feel guilty; free people make others free. And you can always tell how guilty a person feels by noticing how guilty you feel around him or her. Can I repeat that? You can always tell how guilty a person feels by noticing how guilty you feel around him or her. Jesus has made you free. It is important that you bring others to Him for the same surgery that He has performed on you.

As you seek to share with others the joy of your freedom, here are some things to keep in mind. Think of them as tools in your toolbox, to assist you in the job of helping others break out of their prisons:

First, freedom *sees clearly*. A friend of mine has just left the ministry. It has been a very hard time for him. The church he served had such control over him that he came very close to a nervous breakdown. The institutional demands and coercive pressures were horrible. I asked him what he thought about the church and he said, "Steve, it represents everything about the church that I abhor. Everything I hate."

I said, "Jim, when you understand that you were just like them, then you will be free."

There's no sin, dear friend, of which I am not capable. There is no hurt from which I could not suffer. There is no brother or sister in Christ over which I can claim superior goodness. You can't either. One of the great things about being free, knowing that you're forgiven and accepted, understanding grace, is that you don't have anything to protect anymore. When you become free you become able to look at the world and other people as they really are. And once you understand them, you'll be surprised at the compassion you will feel for them.

Not too long ago, as I began to learn something about freedom, I got an eleven-page paper from a man who was trying to correct my theology. His comments were narrow and mean; every sentence was punctuated with a Bible verse taken out of context. I love those kinds of letters and could hardly wait to respond.

Then the Father interrupted my musings on the caustic letter I was going to write. He said, "Stephen, tell him I love him."

And I said, "How can You love him?"

And He said, "I do. Tell him so."

And I said, "Couldn't I tell him that You love him *even if he's wrong*?"

The Lord said, "Just tell him I love him."

Then I got a picture of what this man was going through. I remembered a staff member one time angrily telling me that, if I didn't get off my Calvinistic hobby horse, I was going to destroy the church. I remembered all the letters I had written like the one this man had written to me. I wrote them because of my insecurity, my abandonment issues, and my guilt. Would it have made a difference if someone had told me that God loved me? Well, maybe.

I began to see this man as insecure, afraid, and terribly guilty—not sure that God was in charge, so he had decided to help Him out a bit. I think he also had some serious family and business problems.

So, I simply wrote him a note and said, "Sir, thanks for your letter. I prayed about it and I prayed for you too, and the Father told me to tell you that He loves you a whole lot."

No, I didn't get a response, but I'll bet you that he either got angry or repented. And for the first time, I understood clearly.

Second, freedom *forgives easily*. I have a friend who just left his wife and three children. He's gone through some very serious business problems. He was an upstanding church and community leader. His name was on the letterhead of some very prominent Christian organizations. Then he blew it. I was angry and decided that he needed some strong confrontation.

Then I remembered his father, who was a drunk and had abused him. I thought about the Christian school he had attended, where they gave him nothing but rules and discipline. I thought about his sense of failure and guilt. And then I forgave him, knowing that I was capable of doing everything he had done and more.

Remember Jesus' words to the prostitute:

"Therefore I say to you, her sins, which are many, are forgiven, for she loved much. But to whom little is forgiven, the same loves little." Then He said to her, "Your sins are forgiven." (Luke 7:47–48)

Do you think that she had a problem forgiving after that? Do you think she looked down her nose at anyone anymore? She had been a whore, and she had been forgiven. I'm no better than she was and neither are you.

Let me give you a principle: There is a direct correlation between a lack of forgiveness and a lack of self-knowledge. When you know yourself, you will forgive. I have become friends with a man in California who is a builder—all because of one encounter. I met him in a radio station where he was on the board. After I had done a two-hour interview program, he was standing in the lobby with some other Christians. Someone made a very cutting comment about one of the television evangelists, and I looked at this stranger and noticed that he didn't laugh.

I said to him, "John, how do you feel about that?"

He said, "Steve, it could have been me. Our brother needs our prayers, not our condemnation."

Diogenes blew out his lamp and went home, and the angels sang!

Third, freedom *permits quickly*. When I left the Key Biscayne Presbyterian Church, they had a reception and gave Anna and me a book in which the people of the church had written letters. I will treasure those letters more than you know. But let me brag a little. Over and over again people said, "Steve, thanks for giving me the permission to be free." Well, that church gave me the permission to be free, too. There were bad things I said, mistakes I made, and failures I experienced there. And each time I was loved and accepted and given permission by the church to say bad things, make mistakes, and fail again.

I have an explosive temper and I'm not proud of it. One night at a meeting of the elders, I left the room while they made a very controversial decision with which I strongly disagreed. As soon as they made the decision they fled, sending the youngest elder back to my study to tell me about it! I remember that young man backing up and knocking over a lamp in my study as he, for the first time, experienced my anger. After telling him what I thought, I started systematically making the rounds of the other elders' homes. One elder stood on the porch as I yelled at him. He was in his pajamas. He said, "Pastor, you gonna say the same thing to the other elders?"

And I said, "Doggone right. I just haven't got to them yet."

"Now, pastor, you need to calm down," he said. "I understand you and I love you. You've yelled at me a lot. But some of them are new elders and they're gonna be hurt."

I then went to the home of an elder who is now chairman of the Key Life board. We stood and talked in his living room. He had a German shepherd and he said later that the shepherd went over and hid under a table.

Another elder had already gone to bed. By then I had calmed down anyway and decided to wait until the next morning. But on the way home I got angry again. When I got home I picked up the phone, woke him up and yelled at him.

The next morning every one of those elders called me and told me that they loved me. The chairman of our board called up and said, "Hello, slugger."

You see, they gave me permission to be free and in turn I gave them permission to be free. That's what the relationships between Christians ought to do. Usually, we're playing games. I'm afraid to say anything around you lest you think I'm not very spiritual, and you're exactly the same way with me. So we go through life pretending to believe stuff we don't believe, pretending to live lives we don't live, and pretending to hold opinions we don't hold. May God have mercy on us.

It all begins with one person giving another permission to be free. "I've decided that I'm not going to be critical of you anymore. I'm not your mother and you have my permission to be free." Now, that doesn't mean that we're unaccountable to each other, but I'm not going to dump on you—because it's hard for someone like me to dump on someone like you.

Fourth, freedom *commits responsibly*:

Bear one another's burdens, and so fulfill the law of Christ. (Galatians 6:2)

I believe in accountable relationships, and I believe that those relationships ought to be very honest and very vulnerable. However, because they're so honest and so vulnerable, you can't have very many of them.

Without a commitment that is loving, accountable, and honest, you're not responsible for your brothers and sisters and their walk with God. When one of the children in the Chronicles of Narnia would ask about one of the other children, Aslan would say, "Child, you were only given to know your own story." That's true. And unless I know your story I don't have the right to control your life; nor do I need to let you control mine.

It's important that there be those relationships where people are accountable to each other, but there shouldn't be very many of them. And those kinds of relationships still should allow each person to be free.

I have one of those relationships with a brother, Rusty Anderson, who is a stockbroker in Mobile, Alabama. A few years ago he called me, and at the time there was a deacon sitting in my study. I picked up the phone and said, "Rusty, it's good to hear from you. What's the Lord teaching you?"

There was a dead silence on the other end of the phone, and then a laugh. "You turkey!" Rusty said. "You turkey! Someone's sitting there, and whoever it is you're trying to impress him or her with this spiritual nonsense."

As soon as the deacon left, Rusty and I laughed. And then we "got down" as we discussed my hypocrisy.

A number of years before that, I had been offered the

presidency of a seminary. Billy Graham had called me about it, and the thing was so far out in left field, so wild, that I thought it just might be God's will. I went somewhere on a speaking engagement and took two letters with me. One letter accepted the position and the other withdrew my name from consideration. I honestly didn't know which letter I would send.

Well, Rusty tracked me down. The phone rang in the hotel room. There was no hello, just Rusty's gruff voice. "What are you—crazy? Who in the world told you that you could run a seminary? Are you out of your mind? God didn't call you to raise money and run a school of theology, Steve. You don't even know how to spell *existential*."

Now you know which letter I sent! Rusty is honest. He loves me. He gives me the permission to be free, but he holds my feet to the fire and I do the same for him. We have found grace in our relationship.

Find a brother or sister. Give them the permission to be free. If God deepens the relationship—and only if God deepens it—give them your soul, too.

While speaking at a conference in California a number of years ago, I saw a woman coming across the yard. She absolutely grabbed me in her arms, and I said, "Lady, I never saw you before. Leave me alone."

"I know," she said. "Eddie Waxer told me to do this—and he told me you wouldn't like it!"

A year later I came back to the same conference. The same lady came across the yard and once again hugged me. Then she stepped back and said, "Steve, you're growing! You didn't wince as much as before!"

Well, I've learned that I need people, and there are some people that I need a lot—and I need to be accountable to them.

Freedom for the World

As we put wheels on our freedom, we'll also find it bringing a new sense of purpose to our relationships with the world of unbelievers. Someone tells about Uncle John Vasser, who often witnessed to the folks on Beacon Hill in Boston. One day he witnessed to one of the "social set" ladies, and that night at dinner she told her husband about it. "Dear," she said, "You wouldn't believe what happened to me today!"

"What happened?" he asked, raising up his *Wall Street Journal*.

"A man—a perfect stranger—came up to me and asked if I was a Christian."

"My dear," her husband said, "if I had been there I would have told him to mind his own business."

"My dear," she replied, "if you had been there you would have seen that it *was* his business!"

It was, you know. We're here for them. We've been called to model for the world that which has been given to us.

Let me tell you why I believe that freedom and grace are so important in our witness. I believe that the greatest hindrance to evangelism in our time is Christians who try to tell pagans how nice their prison is. It's not nice and we've got to quit saying it is.

I've been just as angry as you have been over the way Bible-believing Christians have been portrayed in the press. We're seen as narrow, angry, and critical Pharisees. Doesn't that make you mad? Now let me ask you a question: Where do you think the press gets that view of us? Believe it or not, most pagan media people—and I have worked with them for many years—are not bad people. They're amoral, silly, and superficial, but they are, to be quite honest with you, rather nice. There is no conspiracy to destroy Christians and the Christian faith. There is no group of cigar-chomping media moguls waiting to get us. They are, for the most part, misguided working stiffs looking for a story.

And dear friend, we have accommodated them by giving them the wrong image of Christians. A number of years ago in south Florida, we had a major community battle over gay rights. I was a pastor then and was teaching a class for new members. One of the new members came up to me after the class and said, "Steve, have you heard about the commission meeting tomorrow night? They're making an important decision about gay rights. They're going to open our schools to gays, and we ought to have someone at that meeting. Perhaps you ought to make an announcement."

I decided that an announcement was in order. But to be sure, I asked the elders, who met in my study for prayer just before the services on Sunday. Almost without exception they counseled me to wait. One elder said, "Pastor, I have a funny feeling about this thing. I don't think you should make that announcement."

Another said, "Steve, we ought to have someone there, but I would like to check out the whole issue beforehand."

Well, I took their advice and did not ask people to show up at the commission meeting. On Monday night I saw why the elders had been, I believe, supernaturally led. On the television news reports of the commission meeting, Christians were prominent, and they were bashing the pagans over their heads with their signs. Not only that: When anyone spoke with an opposing viewpoint, the Christians shouted them down. The whole meeting was absolute chaos.

You wonder where pagans get their ideas about what we are like? Now you know. The Bible teaches that Christians are to make Jews jealous. That's our call—to witness to Jews. Mostly, however, we've made them afraid. We've made them mad. We've been called to present a loving and free witness to the world, and mostly we've made them angry and mad and we've got to stop it. We're here for them.

Let's talk about the kind of witness we should have:

First of all, the witness of a free Christian *foregoes manipulation*:

> But we have renounced the hidden things of shame, not walking in craftiness nor handling the word of God deceitfully, but by manifestation of the truth commending ourselves to every man's conscience in the sight of God. (2 Corinthians 4:2)

At a church I once served, we used to witness to people with a survey. Did you ever do that? We would say to folks, "I represent a Christian organization, and we're taking a survey. Could I ask you some questions?" And the last question had to do with Christ. I would like to go back and apologize to those folks! It's an outright manipulation. We threw away the surveys.

We would also show films without telling people that there would be an invitation to receive Christ at the end. You can file that under manipulation too.

There's a difference between manipulation and motivation, and we Christians often fail to see it. Fred Smith defines the difference this way: Motivation is for *our* benefit; manipulation is for *my* benefit.

I hardly ever give invitations at the end of my Bible teaching. Let me tell you why. Once when John DeBrine, host of the radio show "Song Time," was out of town, I was asked to fill in for him at "Youth Time," a gathering of two or three thousand teenagers every other Saturday night. John had quite a reputation for two things. First, taking an offering. Whenever I would go to a meeting where John was speaking, I would take with me only as much money as I had already decided to give.

Another thing John was good at was giving an invitation. Whenever John spoke, lots of young people came forward to receive Christ.

Well, on this occasion I decided that I would get more scalps than John. Norm Evans had given his testimony and I was to give the invitation. I described the crucifixion of Christ in all its details. I brought tears to the young people's eyes. I told them that they were selfish and sinful, and that they were just sitting there in their pews while Christ was willing to die that way for them.

I then asked them to stand up for Christ and come forward. And they came by the hundreds, many with tears streaming down their faces.

"Weren't you pleased with such a great response," you ask?

No, I felt dirty. I wanted to send them back to their seats. I wanted to say, "This is not a movement of God's Spirit—it's the result of my glib tongue. Let me tell you the truth . . ." But it was too late. In our witness, we must be always open, honest, and kind in our words.

We used to have a gathering of atheists and agnostics in my study every Monday night, which we called "Skeptics Forum." And I would say, "Look, the reason I'm taking this time to meet with you is because I want to see you guys become Christians. However, I promise not to lie to you. I promise not to pray over you to your face, or beat you over the head with a Bible. I'll simply tell you the truth as I see it. I'll try to provide honest answers to your honest questions."

Many of those skeptics became Christians—and none of them felt manipulated.

We need to be honest about the cost of following Christ. We need to be honest about our own sin. We need to tell pagans that we aren't witnessing to our own goodness but to His. We need to quit pretending that we have all the answers to all the questions. We need to just live our lives honestly and openly, and then point to Christ.

Don't pretend to be something you aren't. If you do, the pagans will think that the Christian faith is only for good people. That would be a horrible lie. Manipulation comes from the pit of hell and smells like smoke.

Second, the witness of a free Christian *allows* *relationships*:

I wrote to you in my epistle not to keep company with sexually immoral people. Yet I certainly did not mean with the sexually immoral people of this world, or with the covetous, or extortioners, or idolators, since then you would need to go out of the world. (1 Corinthians 5:9–10)

On this rock I will build My church, and the gates of Hades shall not prevail against it. (Matthew 16:18)

Once in a church I served we were involved in an "I Found It" witnessing campaign. We were supposed to list all of our unbelieving friends and start praying for them. I started my list . . . and realized that I didn't know a single pagan for whom to pray. I had so narrowed my relationships that I didn't even have any unbelieving friends. That was a scary revelation. Leaven helps the loaf rise, but if it isn't in the loaf it just sits there. Leighton Ford talks about the "holy huddle." He describes a football game where the players get in a huddle and say, "You know, we are having so much fun and we like each other so much . . . let's just stay in the huddle."

Our proximity—or lack of proximity—to pagans reveals the extent of our insecurity. The farther away we are from them the more insecure we are.

Can I say that again? Our proximity—or lack of proximity—to pagans reveals the extent of our insecurity. The farther away we are from them the more insecure we are. I once spoke at a church in Newark, New Jersey. It was the first time I was ever picked up in a limousine. It was wonderful. I was whisked through the streets of Newark into the worst part of town. Then, suddenly, iron gates were opened up and we drove into this very classy and wonderful church . . . and the gates were closed behind us.

After I had spoken for the banquet, one of the elders asked me what they could do about their dying church. "We have money," he said, "but we don't have people."

I told him, "What you ought to do first is tear down the walls."

Dear friend, you should too.

Third, the witness of a free Christian *fosters equality*:

This is a faithful saying and worthy of all acceptance, that Christ Jesus came into the world to save sinners, of whom I am chief. (1 Timothy 1:15)

Someone has defined the church as a nice, mild-mannered gentleman standing in front of a nice, mild-mannered congregation, telling them how to be nicer and more mild-mannered. May God have mercy on our souls! Witnessing is simply one beggar telling other beggars where to find bread.

I have a friend who, betraying everything she held dear, slept with a pagan businessman. Afterwards, she was devastated. She sat in my study and wept. She said, "Steve, I really betrayed my faith in Christ, to someone who is not a believer."

And I said, "Why don't you tell him so?"

She said, "Say what?"

I said, "Why don't you go and tell him so?"

So she went to him and said, "Bill, last night I was attracted to you and I liked you a lot. But last night I lied to you. Not with what I said but in what I did. I love Christ with all of my heart. He has made my life different. But last night I betrayed Him. Today He forgave me, but I betrayed Him to you, and now I am asking you to forgive me too."

The man was absolutely flabbergasted. Two weeks later he became a Christian.

Christians aren't better, just forgiven. Our concept of witnessing often seems to be that we are good people who are on a crusade to make the world as good as we are. May God forgive us! We're just beggars telling other beggars where we found bread. Your attitude in witnessing is far more important than your words. When your attitude is that you are better than the pagan, that you are part of the chosen elite who will come to tell him or her about Christ, they'll know. Your witness will go nowhere. But when you point to Christ as the Man who has the bread . . . you should be prepared to jump out of the way, because pagans are very, very hungry!

Fourth, the witness of a free Christian *attracts questions*:

> For the weapons of our warfare are not carnal but mighty in God for pulling down strongholds, casting down arguments and every high thing that exalts itself against the knowledge of God, bringing every thought into captivity to the obedience of Christ. (2 Corinthians 10:4–5)

> Be ready to give a defense to everyone who asks you a reason for the hope that is in you. (1 Peter 3:15)

I once debated an atheist on Larry King's show in Miami. He was the president of an atheists' association, and he came to the studio with an armful of books and files. I thought to myself, *I'm in trouble! This man is going to eat my lunch!*

Do you know what happened? I won every argument! On more than one occasion during the debate, my atheist opponent said, "That's a good point. I never thought of that before."

Even Larry King, an agnostic, said at one point, "Steve's question is a good one. Why don't you answer it?"

I could have led the man to Christ right on the air except for my compassion—after all, he made his living by being an atheist!

That day, for me, a myth was shattered. There is a popular myth among Christians about the learned, wise, sophisticated unbeliever who will take my faith away from me. As a matter of fact, that kind of unbeliever doesn't exist.

The Bible is true when it says that, "the fool has said in his heart, 'there is no God'" (Psalm 53:1).

These pagans are wrong. That is a great disadvantage in their arguments. Most of you are afraid to tell pagans what you believe because you assume they will win the argument—while your faith may not be much, it's all you've got and you'd rather not lose it. But the truth of the situation is quite different. Pagans are silly, superficial, and sophomoric in their arguments. The most difficult thing in witnessing to pagans is to keep from saying, "That's the most stupid thing I have ever heard. I can't believe that someone with the brains of a peanut would utter such nonsense."

Rather, you have to say, lovingly, "That's an interesting point."

You don't have to be afraid of any question, because what you believe is true. With that assurance, your attitude should be such that unbelievers will feel free to ask you honest questions.

Indeed, a free Christian ought to live his or her life in such a way that it *creates* questions in the minds of pagans. Are you predictable? Do you always say what is expected? Are you just like every other Christian on the face of this earth—bland and nice? If so, you'll never create questions in the minds of pagans. My mentor, Dr. John Stanton, who is in heaven now, told me once when I was a young pastor, "Never tell people you're a pastor. But if they find out, don't let them be surprised."

Let me put that in layman's terms: Don't broadcast the fact that you are a Christian. But when people find out, don't let them be surprised. When they see your honesty, your freedom, your love, your compassion, your lack of criticism, your acceptance, and they hear your laughter . . . and they find out that you're a Christian . . . they should be able to say, "So, that explains it! Let me ask you some questions."

And that brings us to the final point:

The witness of a free Christian involves lots of *laughter*:

Rejoice in the Lord always. Again I will say, rejoice!
(Philippians 4:4)

We make a big deal in the church about the difference between joy and happiness. "Joy is not affected by circumstances; happiness is." Well, that may be true, but I think we are dichotomizing too much.

As a matter of fact, joy and happiness are very similar. They are both manifested by laughter. The Christian is the only person in the world who has anything about which to laugh. Hermes called the early Christians "children of joy." It was not by accident that C. S. Lewis titled his autobiography *Surprised by Joy*. If you are a sour saint, if you take yourself too seriously, or take anything else except God too seriously, then you have not understood joy.

I love Malcolm Muggeridge. His *Jesus Rediscovered* is one of the finest spiritual autobiographies of our time. He was probably the best-known personality in Britain in his day—a television commentator and long-time editor of *Punch* magazine. I remember seeing him on William F. Buckley's show, "Firing Line." His eyes would twinkle as he said some of the most horrible things you've ever heard about the end of Christendom and civilization. Do you know why his eyes twinkled? He had a secret—and everyone could see it.

Buckley asked him if he thought the world would ever produce another Solzhenitsyn. Muggeridge replied, "If the world were encased in concrete, there would be a crack. And out of the crack would grow a flower, and out of the flower would come the voice of Solzhenitsyn."

Let me put that another way: If the world were encased in concrete, there would be a crack. And out of the crack would grow a flower. And out of the flower would come laughter—the laughter of the redeemed.

The best way I know of to witness is to laugh. When they ask you why you're laughing, tell them why.

Remember the slave who decided to bond himself to his master, and allowed the master to put a hole through his ear, signifying that he had chosen slavery? The essence of Christian witness is, if you will, showing people the hole in your ear . . . and then telling them where you got it.

Notes

[1]C. S. Lewis, *The Last Battle* (New York: Macmillan, 1956), 146.

[2]Calvin Miller, *The Singer* (Downers Grove, Ill.: InterVarsity,1975), 143.

[3]Stephen Brown, *When Being Good Isn't Good Enough* (Nashville: Thomas Nelson, 1990).

[4]Dan B. Allender, *The Wounded Heart* (Colorado Springs: NavPress, 1990).

[5]C. S. Lewis, *The Silver Chair* (New York: Macmillan, 1953), 17.

[6]Stephen W. Brown, *Welcome to the Family* (Old Tappan, N. J.: Fleming H. Revell, 1990), Introduction. (Originally published in 1972 as *So Now You Are a Christian*.)

[7]M. Basil Pennington, *Centered Living: The Way of Centering Prayer* (New York: Doubleday, 1986).

[8]Sherwood E. Wirt, *Not Me, God* (Palm Springs, Calif.: Ronald N. Haynes, 1981).

[9]Stephen W. Brown, *Where the Action Is* (Old Tappan, N. J.: Fleming H. Revell, 1971).

[10]John Wenham, *The Goodness of God* (Downers Grove, Ill: InterVarsity, 1974).

[11]Frederick Buechner, *Telling Secrets* (San Francisco: HarperCollins, 1991).

[12]Emily Dickinson, quoted in *The Poems of Emily Dickinson*, ed. Martha Bianchi and Alfred Hampson (Boston: Little, Brown, 1937), 15.

[13]Richard Selzer, *Mortal Lessons: Notes on the Art of Surgery* (New York: Simon and Schuster, 1978), 45.

[14]George Gilder, *Wealth and Poverty* (New York: Basic, 1981).

[15]John Bunyan, *The Pilgrim's Progress* (London: J. M. Dent and Sons, 1967), 222.

[16]Archimandrite Sophrony, *His Life Is Mine*, trans. Rosemary Edmonds (Crestwood, N. Y.: St. Vladimirs, 1977), 73.

General Index

Scripture Index